Breakthroughs

Breakthroughs

Women of the Bible
for
Women Today

Constance Ridley Smith

authorHOUSE·

AuthorHouse™
1663 Liberty Drive
Bloomington, IN 47403
www.authorhouse.com
Phone: 833-262-8899

P. O. Box HM 1928
Hamilton HMHX
Bermuda
441-505-1928
www.breakco.com
info@breakco.com

Published by AuthorHouse 10/09/2020

ISBN: 978-1-4634-1321-7 (sc)
ISBN: 978-1-4634-1320-0 (e)

Library of Congress Control Number: 2011909126

Print information available on the last page.

Any people depicted in stock imagery provided by Thinkstock are models, and such images are being
used for illustrative purposes only.
Certain stock imagery © Thinkstock.

This book is printed on acid-free paper.

Scripture quotations are from The Holy Bible, Authorized King James Version (KJV), Crown
Reference Edition, Copyright 1985 by Holman Bible Publishers, Nashville.

Women of . . .
Faith
Hope
Love
Wisdom
Joy

Compiled First Edition

www.breakco.com

Contents

Love

Wisdom

Acknowledgements

Erma J. Todd and Mrs. Emancia Outerbridge provided very thorough copyedit and critique.

Ashley Chérie Smith and Courtney Amber Smith were valuable editorial assistants, providing both word processing and copyediting.

Larry Smith, Bible enthusiast, added historical perspective and Biblical cross reference. His contribution added balance to many of my purely academic notions.

Other Graphics by Lisa Bardgett and Sandray Fostin.

Foreword

Those of us who are "churched" often use descriptors, lingo, and language that is common among ourselves. Our association with other believers and frequent contact with Bible scholars enhance our knowledge. We thereby gain the ability to quickly recite Bible facts, scriptures, and Bible stories. By mid-life, the themes of the Bible are common knowledge to us. We often assume that they are 'givens' for everyone else, as well.

It can be said that I have studied the Bible more consistently than I have studied any other book in any other discipline. Although I have been involved in many academic programs and have attained degrees and certifications, my research of the Bible has been more far-reaching. I have routinely used research and cross-reference tools to decipher Biblical meaning and translation tools to assist me in understanding Hebrew and Greek word origins. As a practice, I lean toward the King James Version for my personal devotions. Yet in my leisure, I enjoy reading selected passages in the modern romance languages.

Those who speak the language of the Bible as I have described, sometimes struggle to keep their Biblical presentations sequential, free of "presumed common knowledge," understandable, and useful to wider audiences.

To address this issue, I have included discussion starters, questions, and other formats that will allow the reader to make these Bible topics applicable to daily life.

I thank Mrs. Emancia Outerbridge, not only for providing a final copyedit, but also for prompting me to fully explain Biblical terms, the language of the "churched" and other potentially esoteric concepts, thereby keeping this series practical and grounded in ordinary language.

Ms. Erma Todd provided the initial copyedit and encouraged me to continue.

Courtney Amber Smith was a valuable editorial assistant, providing both word processing and copyediting.

Larry Smith, Bible Scholar, contributed to this publication by discussing Biblical ideas and historical facts, thereby adding balance and perspective to many of my purely academic notions.

Pastor Ulric Hetsberger provided a content review of the chapter entitled Women of Hope and prompted me to clarify the concept of destiny. During one of his powerfully insightful sermons, he also introduced me to the Bible Character Rizpah.

This book represents the fruit of my Christian walk from 2006-2013. It represents the ebbs and flows in my experience, my reflection upon them, and God's faithfulness to me.

Constance Ridley Smith
December 22, 2013.

Faith

Sometimes, despite "name-it-and-claim-it" faith, disease takes its ravaging course and a person succumbs to mortality. Does this mean that the believer did not have enough faith?

Or despite continuing echoes of faith, a debilitating condition does not continue to improve. Like medicine after its shelf-life, did that person's faith lose its efficacy?

The journey through illness is a faith walk. When that journey leads to a complete restoration of physical health, we are pleased. When it leads a person to salvation, God is pleased. In some cases, the journey leads to both.

In this section, we will:

- explore the cause of disease and illness
- discuss the healing power of touch
- examine the Five Traits of those who were healed by Christ
- show how women and men of faith followed this plan as they sought healing, and
- discover what these people did as a result.

The Five Traits of those Who Were Healed by Christ
Faith . . . . Humility . . . . Importunity . . . . Obedience . . . . Ministry

Women of Faith
Journey to Wellness

Faith is total reliance upon God. It is based on tenacious conviction and belief in God. Despite evidence to the contrary or what appears on the surface, a Christian believes in the power of God to accomplish His will on earth. When our will is aligned with the will of God, we can watch Him do the impossible on our behalf.

Faith, therefore, is more about bringing man's will into harmony with God's will than it is an exercise whereby man can cajole and convince God to do something other than His perfect will. The Lord's prayer sums it up quite nicely, "Thy will be done on earth, as it is in Heaven" (Matthew 6:10).

The Bible discusses faith from many points of reference. We remember Peter's lack of faith when he tried to walk on water as Christ had done. Through his lacking, we understand that our faith will fail when we depend on our own strength and take our eyes off of the Master.

Faith can be readily understood by reflecting upon the ministry of Christ as he healed and restored men and women of the Bible. Because of their belief in Him, the goodness and virtue that was His to share, and the love exchanged between them, they were healed. In their healing process, they each demonstrated faith, humility, importunity, and obedience. Their response to Him was ministry.

While the primary focus of this book will be the women who were healed by Jesus, these five traits—Faith, Humility, Importunity, Obedience, and Ministry-will form the framework of this chapter on "Women of Faith." These five traits were common to all who were healed by Jesus, men and women alike.

In this book, you will read about a woman whose strength was restored and others who were delivered from demons and infirmities which included a curved spine, an issue of blood, high fever, and an unclean spirit. One was even raised from the dead. These accounts are found in the Gospels of Mathew, Mark, Luke and John. We will make reference to all four of these books of the Bible in our discussion because sometimes one writer of the Gospel has included information or given a perspective that is not found in the other three books.

All four of these Gospels are intriguing, however, it is the book attributed to Luke that helps us to recognize all the branches of medicine that Jesus practiced. In fact, in some circles, Luke is commonly referred to as the New Testament physician. The book of Luke is like a medical journal found in the Bible between the books of Mark and John. The following outline of the book of Luke will show the branches of medicine that Jesus practiced. This outline may also become helpful when you want to cross reference these stories of healing later, in your own studies.

Here is a quick overview of Luke's medical journal, by chapter:

Luke tells about the pregnancies of Elisabeth and Mary in chapter 1; the neonatal and pediatric care of the young Christ child in chapter 2; and the genealogy of Christ in chapter 3. Luke speaks of general healings in chapters 4 and 6. Leprosy, palsy, dropsy, foaming at the mouth, crying out, plagues, demon possession, and blindness were cured in chapters 5 and 6. Chapter 8 mentions Mary Magdalene, a forgiven woman, who was healed of seven diseases. It also mentions Joanna, Susanna and many other women who were healed. Chapter 8 also notes how a woman's 12-year menstrual flow was stopped; ending with Jairus' daughter who was raised from her deathbed. Nutritional needs were met as Christ fed the five thousand in Chapter 9. He gave lessons on stress management to Martha in Chapter 10 and to the disciples in Chapter 12. He cast out devils in Chapter 11; orthopedics and neurology were balanced by psychiatry in Chapter 13, as Jesus cured the woman in the bowed down condition. Ten lepers (dermatology) and a blind man (ophthalmology) were cured in Chapters 17 and 18 and in another book, Jesus compounded and dispensed his own medicines (pharmacology).[1] What a clinic! When Jesus showed up, healing took place.

In addition to the women that Luke named, we find several other women (and men) who were cured by Jesus. Both Matthew and Mark wrote about Simon Peter's mother-in-law who was cured of a high fever and the daughter of a Gentile woman who got rid of an unclean spirit.

The condition and the healing process of each of those who were healed has been my source of inspiration and guidance. Because of their stories, I know that I can claim the healing and delivering power of Jesus Christ. I also know that my response to healing must be ministry.

From a Biblical perspective we will:

- explore the cause of disease
- analyze the meaning of the word "disease"

- discover whether a disease can be caused by an evil spirit
- ponder the question, "Where do demons and evil spirits come from?"
- find out how can we break the strongholds of evil spirits in our lives
- determine who has the power to deliver us from illness and diseases
- study the Five Traits of those who were healed by God

What caused their diseases?

We have mentioned Mary Magdalene, Simon Peter's mother-in-law, Jairus' daughter, the daughter of a Gentile woman, the woman with the issue of blood, and another woman who had a curvature of the spine. Each of these sick women either suffered from a lack of strength, or they were afflicted by a demon or an evil spirit. From my study, I have concluded that both of these causes of infirmity are basically the same as modern-day diseases. In fact, the two English language words, infirmity and disease, are derived from the same Greek word, asthenia.

Chart 1 below illustrates this.

The GREEK WORD Asthenia is the same as...	The ENGLISH WORDS lack of strength...	And the ENGLISH WORD... Disease
Asthenia= (Sthenos)=	Lack of strength= (Strength)=	Disease (Health)
Comment: In Vine's Expository Dictionary, the word infirmity is said to be the Greek asthenia, which literally means "lack of strength" as opposed to sthenos, which means "strength". As such, the Bible promise of II Corinthians 12:9 takes on a deeper meaning, when applied to our health conditions... in His sthenos, we see our asthenia, not just our weakness, but our condition, caused by our lack of strength. That is, our illness or disease.		

Can disease be caused by an evil spirit?

When I was a teacher, students always complained about having to take algebra. They would ask, "Why do I need to take algebra anyway? How will algebra help me in my everyday life?" Or, "When am I going to use this in real life?" they would complain.

Today we're going to use the logic of algebra to probe the relationships between diseases and their probable causes.

In algebra, there is a formula that states:

If a=b
And b=c,
Then a=c
Using this logic:

If evil spirits are sometimes demonic in nature
And demons can cause diseases
Then there is also a relationship between demonic, unclean spirits and diseases.

Algebraic logic can also be applied as follows:

If asthenia is a word used for illness,
And asthenia simply means a lack of strength, then some illnesses are simply caused by a lack of strength that is related to some body part or body system that is not functioning up to par.

In Mark 7:25, a Gentile Woman sought healing for her daughter. The scripture that recounts the story of this Gentile Woman (also called Canaanite/Greek/Syrophoenician) says that the woman's daughter had an unclean spirit. In the Greek language, this use of "spirit" is the word *"pneuma,"* translated, breath—the living breathing part of a human being. (Incidentally, the text uses the word "spirit" with a lowercase "s"). The mother came to Jesus and asked Him to cast the uncleanness (devils) out of her daughter. A look in Vine's *Expository Dictionary of Biblical Terms* shows that the word used in this scripture for unclean is the Greek word "daimonion," the same Greek word that is used for devils, and is a cognate of (sounds like) our present-day word, demon. Spirit (pneuma) is coupled with the word for unclean (daimonion). The essence of this text is that the woman's daughter had foul thoughts, moral reasoning, and activities. Refer to Chart 2 as you consider these facts about daimonion, demons, and devils.

Chart 2 below illustrates this.

The GREEK WORD Daimonion is the same as…	The ENGLISH WORD Demon	And the ENGLISH WORD "spirit," written in the Bible with the lowercase "s."
Daimonion	Demon	(evil) spirit
Comment: When the Bible refers to the type of spirit that causes diseases, "spirit" is often preceded by the words "evil" or "unclean" and, typically, is written with a lowercase "s." It is typically a translation of the Greek word, daimonion.		

A daimonion acts on the power of Satan, as illustrated in Revelation 16: 13-14:

> And I saw three unclean spirits like frogs, out of the mouth of the Dragon and out of the mouth of the beast and out of the mouth of the false prophet for they are the spirits of devils . . .

A daimonion can affect either the body or the mind with disease:

> For a certain woman whose young daughter had an unclean spirit heard of Him and came and fell at His feet (Mark 7: 25).

> While Jesus was preaching in a synagogue, and behold there was a woman which had a spirit of infirmity 18 years, and was bowed together, and could in no wise lift up herself (Luke 8:2).

In scripture, the words evil spirit and infirmities are often paired together:

> And certain women, which had been healed of evil spirits and infirmities, Mary called Magdalene, out of whom went seven devils . . . (Luke 8:2)

> While Jesus was preaching in a synagogue, and behold there was a woman who had a spirit of infirmity 18 years, and was bowed together, and could in no wise lift up herself. (Luke 13:11)

Luke 13:11 explains that while Jesus was preaching in a synagogue, a woman who had a spirit of infirmity came in. Her body was in a bowed down condition. She had been in this condition for eighteen years. The Bible describes the woman as a daughter of Abraham (Luke 13: 16), a term used for a woman who was a believer. This suggests that there may be women in the church who have the same conditions, ailments and issues as women outside of the church. It affirms that illness can affect a woman's quality of life.

Vine's *Expository Dictionary* goes on to say that the bowed down condition, in a modern way of looking at it, was a curvature of the spine. Dr. Luke's diagnosis showed no physical reason behind the curvature. In fact, he called it a "spirit of infirmity," meaning being caused by a spirit. The spirit was of Satan (verse 16) and apparently affected the woman's mental, spiritual, or emotional outlook, causing her to be bowed over. Some translations call the spirit a demon.

It is only through the Light of the World that we can discern the spiritual aspect of a condition or infirmity. In Christ's perfection we see our imperfection. In the Prince of Peace we notice our lack of peace. In His strength, we see our brokenness.

Vine concludes that this correlation of the women's infirmity with a spirit could have only been written by someone qualified as a medical practitioner. Vine's statement supports the opinion that Luke was indeed a physician.

Our Hope for Healing Lies in Our Redeemer

When debilitating illness comes upon us we, like this woman, will not be able to do anything to rise above the condition ourselves (Read Luke 13:11). Our deliverance will be accomplished *only* by a Power greater than our own.

The inability to help oneself was also the condition of the woman who had an issue of blood for twelve years.

The Book of Mark states:

> And a certain woman had an issue of blood for 12 years and had suffered many things of many physicians and had spent all that she had and had nothing bettered but rather grew worse (Mark 5: 25-26).

The Book of Luke records the same story:

> And a woman having an issue of blood 12 years, which had spent all her living upon physicians, neither could be healed of any, came behind Him and touched the border of His garment: and immediately her issue of blood stanched (Luke 8: 43-44).

A blood flow stopped immediately from a touch? Can this be? This woman had, no doubt, been touched by the many physicians she had visited. Why was she not healed at any other point along the way? Why *this* touch?

Goodness and Virtue. There are two reasons. The first reason is revealed to us in Luke Chapter 6. This chapter opens with several scenarios that reveal the character of Christ. His character is key to understanding the power of His touch. In Christ, there is goodness. He has power against the illnesses caused by evil spirits, because He is good. In short, the antidote for evil spirits caused for Satan is to seek the goodness of our Lord and Saviour. Before we discuss how to seek the Goodness and Virtue of Christ, let us probe Luke Chapter 6 to establish the character of Christ, with respect to healing.

Luke 6 is written to show us the motivation of Christ, which was and is now, to do good in the lives of others. In Luke 6, Christ had been criticized for allowing his disciples to pluck and eat corn on the Sabbath day and healed a man's withered hand on another Sabbath day. His response to the critics (the scribes and the Pharisees) was "Is it lawful on the Sabbath days to do good, or to do evil? To save life, or to destroy it?" Further in the chapter, Christ went into a mountain to pray all night. After he came down from the mountain, He and His disciples stood in an open spot of land, a plain. A great multitude of people came to the plain. They came from Judea, Jerusalem, Tyre, and Sidon to hear Him and be healed of their diseases. The second reason why the touch of Christ was a healing touch is revealed in verse 19:

> . . . came to hear him and be healed of their diseases; And they that were vexed with unclean spirits: and they were healed. And the whole multitude sought to touch him: for there went virtue out of him, and healed them all.

Likewise, when the woman with the issue of blood touched the hem of His garment, His virtue went out of Him and healed her. The remedy for the evil spirits that Satan sends to create illness in our minds, emotions, and, consequently, our bodies is to pray and seek to come into the presence of his virtue. In order to be healed of *daimonion* and evil spirits, *we must seek Christ*. Although we can no longer physically touch Him or His garments, we can come apart, commune, pray, meditate, and daily, hourly, or each minute of the day, as it is necessary, and ask Him for strength to overcome. Healing comes as we call upon Him to help us to overcome the evil spirits that bind us. Our healing may not be immediate, but each call to Christ is like a dose of Divine medicine. It builds our connection to Him as the Healer and creates an exchange that will, in fact, bring us healing and victory over the evil spirits that bind us in illness and emotional distress.

In this life many things can happen to us. Sometimes we are exposed to the power of evil messages or spirits by what we see; the trauma or losses that we experience; gruesome events that we witness; how people treat us in relationships; or information that we come into contact with. In this century, information is literally exploding into our homes and into our personal space—by way of television, internet, music, and people that Satan employs as his agents. Sometimes these messages produce compulsive behaviors, addictions, and haunting within our minds that can control or debilitate us and the ones we love. Our response to these messages can even make us physically ill. The antidote is to seek goodness and the virtue of Christ.

Go to a quiet place, a cabin in the mountains, a cottage by the sea, or a sanitarium or wellness facility, if you can afford it. Remove yourself from the toxic environment and people that cause you emotional harm. The barest furniture, fewest articles of clothing, limited amounts of outside media for a period of time can work wonders for helping to restore your connection to His Goodness and Virtue.

If you cannot afford any of these retreats, find a hiking trail, a park, a special tree or a special place in nature where you can commune with God and feel the solitude that is necessary to bring healing. It is likely that one spot will become your favorite. Create a routine by selecting appointed times that you will visit your selected spot. Incorporate other rituals that are pleasing to you. When you reach that spot, you might open your thermos and enjoy a cool, refreshing drink of water from it. Open your Bible or devotional and read a passage. Rehearse the Gems of Faith that are found at the end of this chapter.

What ever your economic means are, God is available to you to heal you and to restore your health and well being.

Love. Healing comes from a *loving* touch—by someone you love and believe in and someone who you know loves and tenderly cares about you. In fact, that is why many health advisors tell those who are sick to "find a physician that you can believe in." To that counsel, I might also add, find one whose philosophy on life and dying matches your own."

Both women we have discussed, the one in the bowed down condition and the woman with the issue of blood, determined Christ to be such a physician. They had faith in His power to heal them. But they loved Him. Without love for Him, his touch would have not had the power to dispel their disease. We can agree on one point: if you are repulsed by someone, the last thing you want is for them to touch you.

After I wrote the book, *Mothers of Faith*, upon which this chapter is based, I was contacted via email by a young woman who suffered from a skin condition, like eczema. She told me that for several years she was in a scratch-itch cycle, scratching so much until her skin was raw and would often bleed. Like the woman with the issue of blood she was also anemic, but she could not stop the scratch-itch ritual. It controlled her life. She would get the urge to scratch and would not stop until it bled. It was unsightly and all who saw this area of her skin were mortified. The young woman went from doctor to doctor, spending all she had (in a sense) on office visits, biopsies, labs, blood tests. There was no physical reason for her skin condition. It was not bacterial, viral, pathogenic, nor contagious. The last physician she visited told the woman, "The cause of this thing is not known." Another physician queried the woman, "what is bothering you?" The woman began to recall a litany of pressures caused by the cares of life, trauma, bad relationships, abuse, death of loved ones and an encounter with pornography that made her feel dirty and ashamed. She withdrew from all intimacy and literally began to hate the perpetrators of her abuse. Over a period of time, she sought God for healing and through counseling, reading, and living in harmony with the laws of nature, she found some relief. But one evening in a retreat setting, she experienced the turning point in her recovery. As the group was in a prayer circle, holding hands, she began to feel, for the first time, in a very long time love and its transforming power. She described to me an uplifting feeling that helped her, in time, to overcome the hatred that had bound her for years. Every time she remembered the hatred, the abuse, the loss, the trauma, the shame, or the guilt, she replaced those images with the image of the warmth she experienced that night in the prayer circle.

Within a few months, she was able to stop the compulsive scratching. Her outlook improved. The raw skin healed and her emotions began to follow suit. The young woman claimed the promise found in Psalm 147:3:

He healeth the broken in heart, and bindeth up their wounds.

Healing is often attached to closeness, both physical and emotional. For example, when David was stricken with old age, they brought a young maid to lie next to him (I Kings 1:1-4). When the prophet Elijah was called upon to heal the widow's son, he laid his body on the body of the lad(II Kings 4:35). That is part of our human condition—the need for closeness. People fare better in the hospital and recuperating from surgery when they have family support. They gain power over diseases and habits when they are affiliated with a support group.

On the other hand, however, we can become swept away with the notions that arise out of our thought life. In these instances, our resulting desire for closeness defies logic. As an aside, I'd like to share with you a true story about how one woman's desire for closeness defied logic.

Without a doubt, my favorite spectator sport is basketball. I grew up hearing the squeak of rubber soles on parquet. You can imagine the joy I felt when my husband surprised me with tickets for us to see the New York Knicks play in my hometown. The tickets he purchased gave us seats behind the Knicks team bench. Just as much excitement happens in the stands behind the team as on the floor. At one of the timeouts, one of the "stars" wiped the perspiration from his face and torso with a white towel. He tossed the towel into the stands. A young "twenty-something" caught the towel and proceeded to wipe her own face with the towel and kiss it as if the moist towel were a piece of gold. Her act defied logic. The thought of it will make many of you cringe, but her actions demonstrated how much she loved—at least the idea—of being close to the basketball "star".

The power of loving touch is key to healing, but it is also essential for wellness. I was on the worship committee for our church. Those in charge were trying to figure out a way to shorten the services, which had gotten quite lengthy. The worship leader's suggestion was to trim

> The need for closeness is attached to humanity.

the time by eliminating the greeting. In this particular church the greeting is the period of time where the musicians play lively music and persons can leave their seats and greet and hug others in the congregation. One woman let us know that her aunt, an elderly woman who lives alone, came to church only for that segment of the service. In fact, after the greeting, she rarely returned to her seat. She most often left the service, continuing out the side door, into the parking lot. In other words she came to church for the hugs and "warm fuzzies" that she received during that portion of the service. One elderly gentleman also stated that this was the only time a young woman wearing nice perfume would smile at him and give him a hug.

These stories are probably a bit trite, but they underscore the desire we all have for human touch. In hospital neonatal units, the babies who are cuddled and held thrive; those who are fed and bathed without cuddling fail to thrive. In these ways, we are no different from the woman with the issue of blood.

The woman with the issue of blood associated Christ with love and hope and she was thereby, healed. According to the Bible story, when she grabbed the hem of his garment, she received healing. Yet, the healing power was not in his garment, but in the *love* that she associated with the Christ who wore the garment. It was a transaction that was created in her mind, her spirit, and her emotions. Her healing was created first in her thought life. Similarly, I have also found that the battle for many of our ailments emanates from our thought life and our willingness to rehearse positive messages in one's mind rather than negative ones. For this reason, I have determined to seek love, rather than hate.

A lack of strength also causes disease. Sometimes though, illness does come from a breakdown in the body systems. We are genetically predisposed to certain illnesses by virtue of our family history (our forefathers). In those cases, illness is not caused by a demon, but by a lack of strength or poor functioning within one's body systems. Our lifestyle choices, eating, and exercise habits also contribute. Prolonged stress and our outlook on life can make these conditions flourish. Our reactions to emotional triggers can affect our immune system and our ability to cope. The book, *SuperImmunity*, by Paul Pearsall, Ph.D. makes a similar case about the powerful effect of emotions on one's health. In fact, he suggests that the immune system is controlled by one's self-talk and that there are certain diseases which affect persons who are explosive "hot reactors" and other diseases that befall those who withdraw, who are defeatist in their attitudes, the "cold reactors." These reactions and attitudes can lead to breakdown of body systems and major life illnesses that are characterized by the Greek word, asthenia—a lack of strength.

In this type of illness, the advice to find a physician in whom you can trust to guide your healing process is key to restoring your health. If both you and your physician share beliefs on spiritual matters, wellness, quality of life, longevity, and death, you are more likely to have a healing plan and, perhaps, recovery that is satisfying to you and your family members. If you are a believer and your physician operates in methods that are compatible with Word of God, you will be doubly blessed.

If you want to be healed, surround yourself with those who love you and tenderly care for you.

The remainder of this chapter will talk about many women of the Bible who found their healing. Their stories underline for us what faith in God can do to relieve our suffering. It reminds us that a woman can be a churchgoer, or perhaps, even a member and still find herself crippled by disease. She may not be able to lift herself. She can return home each time as she left home—spiritually low. She can come to church 18 years with a "demon" on her back. She can bleed physically or emotionally for 12 years and see no sign of relief.

What made the difference for these women of the Bible? How can today's woman find healing and deliverance from the demons or spirits of infirmity that bind her mentally, physically, spiritually, or emotionally?

The Five Traits of those Who Were Healed By Christ

The healings performed by Christ are based on His goodness and virtue and the loving touch He rendered. But those that He healed demonstrated five common traits in their healing process. Those Five Traits are:

1. Humility
    (a bowed down condition)
    The Bible illuminates: If my people, which are called by my name, shall humble themselves, and pray, and seek my face, and turn from their wicked ways; then will I hear from heaven, and will forgive their sin, and will heal their land. (II Chronicles 7:14)

2. Faith
   (seeking the word of God or the Word of God)
   The Bible explains: "Faith comes by hearing and hearing
   by the word of God." (Romans 10:27)

3. Importunity[3]
   (doing whatever is necessary to gain healing:
   perseverance, persistence)
   Though he will not rise and give him because he is his
   friend, yet because of his importunity, he will rise and
   give him as many as he needeth. (Luke 11:5-8)

4. Obedience
   (following God's plan for our health, our healing, and for
   our lives)
   Then Peter and the other apostles said, We ought to obey
   God rather than men. (Acts 5:29)

5. Ministry
   (going on God's errands)
   The Bible explains: But I have prayed for thee, that thy
   faith fail not: and when thou art converted, strengthen
   thy brethren. (Luke 22:32)

Demonstration of Faith, Humility, and Importunity

In the pages that follow, we will look at three women of the Bible
and gain an understanding of how they exhibited faith, humility,
and importunity during their journey to wellness. Next, we will
examine and more fully define each of the elements of the Five
Traits.

1. **The Woman with the Issue of Blood
   Had Faith and Demonstrated her Humility**

The woman with the issue of blood came behind Christ and
touched the hem of his garment, which means she must have
been crouched to the ground. This bowed down condition was

the correct position for the woman with the issue of blood to assume in order to receive her deliverance. It symbolized her humility. She was low financially, low emotionally, and ghastly anemic, yet she was spiritually astute enough to know that if she could just grasp the hem of His priestly robe, she could signify to Him that she believed in His Lordship and His power. This act demonstrated her faith. In those days it was commonly known that in the hem, priestly robes were trimmed with a ribbon of blue. The ribbon of blue symbolized Jesus' royalty and Kingship. By grasping for the hem, she knew that she could communicate what she was too weak and low to communicate with words. In an exchange that transcended earthly ears and human understanding, she called Him Lord, my Maker, my Healer, and my Redeemer.

2. **The Woman with the Spine Curvature**
    She was in a Bowed Down Condition and Demonstrated her Faith

A similar dynamic occurred with the woman who had been living in a bowed down condition for 18 years. She was perpetually in the position of humility, a bowed down condition. By making it to the synagogue on the Sabbath day, she proclaimed Him to be Lord of the Sabbath, Lord of creation, and Lord of her deliverance. For the same Lord who preached in the synagogue on the Sabbath, was the same Lord who created her, and could therefore, heal and deliver her. This thinking was based on her belief in the Word of God, her faith.

This woman knew first-hand what Paul would later write in Romans Chapter 10 verse 27: "Faith comes by hearing and hearing by the word of God." Her venture to the synagogue that day would allow her to hear the word of God being read and also to see the Word of God (Jesus), in the flesh.

To fully understand her healing, one must first understand that the Sabbath was ordained as a memorial of the creation week. On it, God rested from His creative activity. On it, we can obtain rest from earthly activity and become rejuvenated for the week ahead. When the ruler of the synagogue saw the woman, he looked at her disdainfully. He saw another poor, wretched soul. When Christ, the ruler of the Sabbath, saw the same woman He saw an opportunity to allow someone else to enjoy the rest, rejuvenation, and renewal that is available to all, each week, on the Sabbath day. This woman courageously made her way to the House of delivery on the day of deliverance. He, being the Lord of deliverance, loosed her bond and glorified God. Hallelujah!

3. **The Syrophoencian Woman**
   Had Humility and Faith; She Demonstrated Importunity

Our third example of healing was the Gentile woman whose daughter had an unclean spirit within her. Perhaps her story is included in the Bible to illustrate the value of "doing whatever it takes to receive that which you seek" (importunity).

It is interesting to note that this woman was a nonbeliever—at least to the human eye. Jesus' words to her, that it is not suitable to take the children's bread and throw it away to the dogs, underscored the fact that He knew that she was a Gentile and potentially, a nonbeliever. However, the fact that she received healing for her daughter shows that Jesus was not an elitist, prejudiced, nor a supremacist. Today, as in those days, His blessings of healing are available to all. He does not limit healing to those who believe in Him.

Her reply to Him, "yet the dogs under the table eat of the children's crumbs," was an acknowledgment of the woman's humility and her submission to His Lordship. Again, as with the other two women who were healed by Christ, the Gentile woman's words were symbolic of a bowed down, low position. Her words 'under the table' and 'eating what only a dog would eat' showed her humility. Her willingness to seek the Savior's healing power on behalf of her daughter showed her faith in Jesus, the Word of God (John 1:1), not as a nonbeliever, but as a believer!

Examining The Five Traits of Those Who Were Healed:

Point 1. "What does it mean to have faith?"

In the face of illness and disease, some people gain strength by reciting a mantra of faith each day. They make statements such as, "I am trusting God to heal me." Their belief is that by saying it, it will come to pass. This is based on the first clause of the Bible verse, Proverbs 18:21, "Death and life are in the power of the tongue: and they that love it shall eat the fruit thereof."

Sometimes, however, despite their "name-it-and-claim-it" philosophy, the disease takes its ravaging course and the person succumbs to their mortality (earthly death).

Or, a person may have a debilitating condition which has a poor prognosis (expectancy for improvement). Initially, the debilitating condition defies the odds and the sufferer shows some indications of miraculous improvement. But despite further echoes of faith, the condition does not continue to improve. Does this indicate that the believer did not have enough faith? Or, like medicine after its shelf-life, did their faith lose its efficacy?

In both instances, the believers exercised faith. But what went wrong? Perhaps there is a difference between what God thinks of as faith, and what man thinks of as faith. In most cases, Jesus responded to the person who was ill by saying "it is done because of your faith," "thy faith has made thee whole," or "go and sin no more." However, the Pharisees criticized Him for mixing the healing of illnesses with the forgiveness of sins. "Who is he," they asked "who has the power to forgive sins?"

The ill person is looking for wellness of the body; Christ is looking for salvation of the soul. The journey through illness is a faith walk. When that journey leads to a complete restoration of physical health, we are happy. When it leads a person to salvation, and what Christ meant by "whole," God is happy. Sometimes the journey leads to both. Sometimes it does not. When it does not, our crowning act of faith must be in the perfect bodies we will have in the earth made new (read Revelation 21:4).

Point Two. What is humility?

In order to be the propitiation for our sins, Christ had to be born as a human and live on earth, among men. The Bible records that He was in all ways tempted as we are tempted today. His willingness to walk among men gave Him first-hand experience about the conditions that we find ourselves trying to manage and overcome. That is why He can minister on our behalf, show us mercy in time of need, and see us through our journey toward wellness.

> "For we have not an high priest which cannot be touched with the feeling of our infirmities; but was in all points tempted like as we are, yet without sin." Hebrews 4:15

> "He is despised and rejected of men; a man of sorrows, and acquainted with grief . . ." Hebrews 53:3

> "He was oppressed and He was afflicted, Yet He did not open His mouth; Like a lamb that is led to slaughter, And like a sheep that is silent before its shearers, so He did not open His mouth." Isaiah 53:7 NAS Version

Likewise, without suffering, we cannot have affinity with Christ, nor can we be in touch with our fellow man. We can better minister to others when we have also shared challenges similar to the ones they face. Our association with the challenges that others face allows us to 'go on God's errands' among our fellow man and to do as Christ would have done.

Point Three. What is importunity?

Another look at the healing journeys of these three women shows one other similarity. We have determined that all three of them demonstrated faith and humility. The third characteristic they shared was their importunity.

Importunity is putting oneself in the position to receive that which one is seeking. In the healing process, importunity is a relentless search for wellness. For the woman with the issue of blood, it meant going to doctor after doctor, literally spending all she had. For the woman who had the curvature of the spine for 18 years, it meant making her way to where Jesus would be on the Sabbath day, at whatever cost. For the Syrophencian or Gentile woman, importunity was reaching across cultural biases to get what was needed for her daughter. All three women put themselves in the position to receive the blessing of healing.

Importunity is explained in the Bible through the parable Christ gave to His disciples in Luke Chapter 11: 5-8. In this parable, Jesus tells about one friend who comes to the other friend at midnight seeking food. Christ states that the sleeping man would rise and get food for his friend, not because of friendship, but because of his friend's importunity.

Later on in his book, Luke cites another parable to elaborate upon the concept of importunity. In Chapter 18, Christ speaks of a judge who neither feared God, nor regarded man. As a judge, he was therefore morally unqualified to do the job he was entrusted to do. Christ disqualified this judge based on the two key attributes necessary for the position. His illustration shows the effectiveness of the widow's importunity in getting what she sought from the judge. If the judge had feared or reverenced God, he would have avenged the woman of her enemy based on the law of the Ten Commandments. If he had regarded man, he would have avenged the woman based on the Two Great Commandments recorded in the book of Matthew Chapter 1. But because he neither regarded man, nor feared God, the woman's importunity was the key. Luke 18: 5 summarizes in this way:

> Yet because this widow troubleth me, I will avenge her, lest by her continual coming she weary me. And shall not God avenge his own elect, which cry day and night unto Him, though He bear long with them? I tell you

> that he will avenge them speedily. Nevertheless when
> the Son of man cometh, shall He find faith on earth?

In summary, importunity can be defined as shameless persistence[3]. It suggests putting oneself in the position to receive because of the expectation to receive. Importunity implies the requestor's impotence and the grantor's potency. The requestor seizes the opportunity that is before him. For example, the hungry friend put himself at the door of a man with children, a man who was likely to have food in the house. The woman with the spirit of infirmity put herself in the synagogue where Jesus was going to preach. The woman with the issue of blood pressed her way in the crowd behind Jesus, just close enough to touch the border of His garment (Mark 5:27). Simon (and Andrew) petitioned the Lord about Simon's mother-in-law's fever when He came to Simon's house (Mark 1:30). When Jesus departed into the coasts of Tyre and Sidon, the Gentile woman followed Him to ask for healing for her daughter (Matthew 15:21-22). The women healed of evil spirits and infirmity in Luke 8:2 got to Jesus by pressing their way to Him when He came into their midst. This is importunity.

Point Four. Obedience

The fourth point of commonality among those who were healed is their obedience. Obedience is trapped in a foible of human nature. We cleverly rationalize against the simplicity of God's health counsel on diet, exercise, and the management of stress. And when we do decide to make changes in our lives, we often make them too late to bring a significant impact on our quality of life and, often, our mortality. We pass the paper/pencil test, but fail the application exercise. Like many, I have scoffed at natural remedies and God's simple plan for healthful living or restoring my health. I've selected the counsel that I believed to be important and de-selected the other. I've often gained knowledge that I didn't incorporate into a lifestyle change. I now conclude that there is no remedy that will help without obedience to the recommended plan. It is not enough to hear and understand. We must apply that knowledge. This is the essence of obedience.

Naaman the leper is a Biblical example which shows the power that is available when we, in obedience, follow the health counsel that has been given to us. Naaman was a highly credentialed man, but he was a leper. His skin condition (leprosy) was a physical illness, but according to Biblical principles, leprosy also indicated a spiritual lacking in Naaman's life. (You may recall that Moses's sister was also plagued with leprosy as a result of her unwillingness to accept Zipporah as Moses's wife).

The remedy that was spoken to Naaman through the prophet Elijah seemed to be a bit extreme. Namaan could not understand the significance of dipping his body into the Jordan River seven times. But it was only upon his full obedience to the prophet's plan that his skin condition was healed.

Whether the counsel is to reduce your consumption of sugar, starches and fried foods; add more fiber to your diet; adhere to a daily exercise routine; or make time for prayer, meditation, and relaxation, it is only through obedience to the counsel that the struggle to regain our health can be won. God's plan wins out over man's.

What is God's plan for our health? What blessings will obedience to God's plan avail for our longevity and our quality of life? Does adherence to God's plan really matter?

Isaiah Chapter 58 contrasts the difference between God's perception and man's. From this passage of scripture, we can deduce that there is a difference between God's perception and man's, generally speaking. To this I offer you, the reader, the same counsel that Paul offered in Acts 5:29:

"We ought to obey God rather than men."

Another Bible text explains it this way: "There is a way that seemeth right unto a man, but the end thereof, are the ways of death (Proverbs 16:25)."

The main theme of Isaiah 58 is God's desire to save his people by pointing out their shortcomings, giving them a plan to achieve oneness with Him, and restoring them to their original purpose—to ride upon the "high places" of life. That is the definition of health. That is good living. And incidentally, that is what we also aspire to, today.

The illustration used in Isaiah 58 centers on the concept of fasting. When we fast for healing, my impression and my experience has been that fasting removes the interference from unhealthy signals so that the body can regulate itself and/or benefit from treatment given to restore one's health.

Fasting breaks the connection between the person and the offensive habit, practice, food, substance, thoughts, or thought patterns. In the absence of interference, the body can, many times, regulate itself.

Fasting is an alignment activity. It's greatest value may not be in the denial of food or substance, but in the opportunity that it provides to restore clear thinking.

But Isaiah 58 is much more than a commentary on the practice of fasting and denying oneself food and drink. The significance of the scripture is that it draws a contrast between what man thinks is appropriate and what God thinks is appropriate. It thereby serves as a guidepost for seeking God's will and obeying it, even in matters related to our health.

At the opening of chapter 58, God asks Isaiah to lift up his voice like a trumpet and show the Israelites (House of Jacob) their sins and transgressions. Through the prophet, they were instructed that their version of fasting was basically inadequate because it served their own purposes and self-directed motives. It didn't make a difference in the way they treated others. Violence and strife were still a part of their lives. In other words, their fast was full of form, but it did not contain substance. To those looking on, it appeared that they were reaching God. But God's counsel was clear,

> "Ye shall not fast as ye do this day to make your voice to be heard on high." (Isaiah 58:4)

In verse 5 God asks them a question, "Is it such a fast that I have chosen?" God further explains that His own fast is one that looses the bands of wickedness, feeds the hungry, and ministers to the poor and less fortunate. In other words, it suggests to us that we may be able to fool others with our pious acts of holiness, but God cannot be fooled. God cannot be mocked, tricked, or hoodwinked into blessing us and healing us. We must be sincere and aligned with His practices and purposes.

God's promise for our obedience to His way of fasting is revealed in verse 8:

> "Then shall thy light break forth as the morning, and thine health shall spring forth speedily: and thy righteousness shall go before thee: the glory of the lord shall be thy reward."

Sometimes health comes when we shift our focus. We can get man's attention by lip-service, adherence to checklists, and busywork. This is obeisance. But only a true commitment to God's precepts can move us from obeisance to obedience. That's what gets God's attention.

When we abandon unproductive behaviours that give the appearance of obedience and begin to truly obey His plan, we can experience His healing.

Point Five. Ministry-Our Response to Miraculous Healing.
Gratitude for healing is a demonstration of thankfulness that is not necessarily audible, but is visible in one's living, one's giving, and the calling upon one's life. To show gratitude, those healed by Jesus followed Him, ministered unto Him, and labored in

His service. A life of service is a more powerful testimony than words uttered before a crowd.

In fact, many times Christ bade those who were healed not to tell anyone. As a result of this study, I noted that Christ did not want the multitudes to see what He did and begin to worship Him prematurely, rather than worship the Father who had sent Him. That would have only served to intensify the anger of the religious zealots who were against Him, already (Mark 9:31). Christ healed and raised people from the dead so that they might go on God's errands and glorify God. This is a template for us. Our mission is to tell others about God's goodness. While it is a good thing to speak your witness, it is better to *be* a witness.

The following chart summarizes the record of faith, humility, and importunity demonstrated by those who sought healing in the Bible. It also shows the resulting ministries of those who were healed. Their obedience is implied.

WOMAN WITH ILLNESS	DEMONSTRATION OF FAITH, HUMILITY, & IMPORTUNITY	EVIDENCE OF MINISTRY
Woman with the Alabaster Box Mark 14:3-9	She found the house where He had been invited to dinner, came there and began to wash and anoint Him.... Christ pronounced to her, "Thy faith has saved thee. Go and sin no more." Luke 7:50	By worshipping Him.... In an act of worship and faith in His ability to save her, she anointed His feet with ointment after washing them with her tears and drying them with her hair. Mark 14:3-9
Women healed of evil spirits and infirmities Luke 8:2	They were healed. Luke 8:2	By ministering....They followed Him throughout every city and village and ministered unto Him with their substance; after the crucifixion, they prepared spices and brought them to the sepulcher. Luke 8:3; 24:1, 10
Jairus' daughter Mark 5: 35-43	Jairus was there waiting for Him (Jesus) to return. Jairus fell down at Jesus feet and asked Jesus to come to his house, even though other people thronged him (scolded him) for doing so. Luke 8:40-41	By living....She lived; and He charged them that no man should know it. Luke 8:56

WOMAN WITH ILLNESS	DEMONSTRATION OF FAITH, HUMILITY, & IMPORTUNITY	EVIDENCE OF MINISTRY
Gentile woman who had a daughter with unclean spirit or devil. Matthew 15:21-22	She followed Him into Tyre and Sidon, and fell at His feet. Jesus told her: "O woman, great is thy faith: be it unto thee even as thou wilt and her daughter was made whole from that very hour." Matthew 15:28	By living a new life.... And He charged them that they should tell no man. Mark 7:36
Woman with a spirit of infirmity for 18 years Luke 13:11	She came to the synagogue where He was preaching on the Sabbath day. Jesus said to her, "Woman, thou art loosed." Luke 13:12	By glorifying God... Immediately she was made straight, and glorified God. Luke13:13
Woman with issue of blood Mark 5:27-34	When she heard of Jesus, she came in the press behind, and touched His garment. For she said, if I may but touch His clothes, I shall be made whole. Jesus told her, "Daughter, thy faith has made thee whole." Mark 5:28, 34	By going in peace, free from illness...She fell down before Him, to which He replied, "Go in peace and be whole of thy plague." Mark 5: 33-34
Mother-in-law with high fever Matthew 8:14	They went to the synagogue and told Jesus that Simon's mother-in-law lay sick. He took her by the hand and lifted her up and immediately the fever left her. Mark 1:29, 31	By ministering... She arose and ministered unto them. Matthew 8:15 Mark 1:31

MAN WITH ILLNESS	FAITH, HUMILITY, & IMPORTUNITY	EVIDENCE OF MINISTRY
Leper Mark 1:40	The leper was beseeching Him (Christ) and kneeling, saying: "If thou wilt, thou can make me clean. Mark 1:40-41 Jesus answered by saying, "I will; be thou clean."	In offerings... See thou say nothing to any man; but go thy way, shew thyself to the priest, and offer for thy cleansing those things which Moses commanded, for a testimony unto them. Mark 1:44
Blind Bartimeus, the beggar Mark 10:46	And when he heard it was Jesus of Nazareth, he began to cry out and say... Have mercy on me. And many charged him to hold his peace, but he cried more a great deal, Thou Son of David, have mercy upon me. Mark 10:47-48 Jesus replied to him, "Go thy way; thy faith has made thee whole." Mark 10:52	By following Jesus... Received his sight and followed Jesus in the way. Mark 10:52
Two Blind Men Matthew 9:28	According to thy faith, be it unto you... See that no man know it.	They spread Jesus' fame and brought someone else to be healed—a dumb man who was also possessed with a devil.
Centurion's servant sick with palsy and grievously tormented Matthew 8:5	I have not found so great faith, no not in Israel... Go thy way; and as thou hast believed, so be it done unto thee. Matthew 8:10,13	Servant was made whole, indi- cating that he continued to minister in his customary way (serving his nation and building synagogues- see Luke 7:5)

MY OWN ILLNESS	DEMONSTRATION OF FAITH, HUMILITY, & IMPORTUNITY	EVIDENCE OF MINISTRY

The Response to Miraculous Healing
Is
Ministry

Build up the Kingdom

BIBLE PROMISES FOR YOU

The effectual, fervent prayer of a righteous man [or woman] availeth much.

James 5:16

Let your light so shine before men that they shall see your good works and glorify your Father, which is in heaven.

Matthew 5:16

Codebreaker Puzzle

Codebreaker

Instructions: The puzzle grid is located on the previous page. In each square of the puzzle grid, put the letter which corresponds to the numeral in the square. For example, write the letter "A" in each square on the grid that contains numeral "1." Write the letter "O" in each square on the grid that contains numeral "2," and so on.

Guess the unknown letters to make a word that refers to a term that is used in this section. There are a few words and abbreviations that are not used in the text, such as:
AO - Alpha and Omega
TI - the seventh syllable of the (solfége) music scale.
ET - French for "and."

Clues:

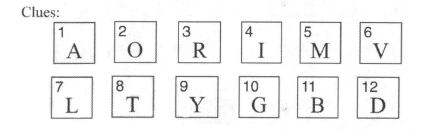

| 1 A | 2 O | 3 R | 4 I | 5 M | 6 V |
| 7 L | 8 T | 9 Y | 10 G | 11 B | 12 D |

Think About It 🗩

1. Have you ever been miraculously healed from an illness?
    _____
    _____

2. What role did faith, humility, obedience, or importunity play in your own healing?

    a. _____
    b. _____
    c. _____

3. How have you shown gratitude for your healing?

    a. _____
    b. _____

4. In what ways have you ministered to others?

    a. _____
    b. _____

5. What is the role of modern-day medicine in today's world? How does it fit into God's plan for healing the sick?
    _____
    _____

The Five Traits Of Those Who Were Healed

Faith . . . . Humility . . . . Importunity . . . . Obedience . . . . Ministry

Faith
Faith puts us in touch with the will of God concerning us.

By reading and hearing His word (the Bible) we learn His will for our lives and more about His ways.

As we pray for the things that are in His will and will bring Him glory, we can be assured that He will supply all of our needs according to His riches in Glory (Philippians 4:19)

Faith should give us the ability to accept whatever the outcomes are. Healing?—okay. No healing? Still okay. Our journey should lead us to an acceptance that God is Sovereign and that He is working all things for our good. (Romans 8:28)

Here are some **"Gems of Faith"** regarding illness and healing. Place a check next to the statements that bring you comfort as you journey toward wellness.

Gems of Faith

- ☐ Beloved, I wish above all things that you will prosper and be in good health, even as thy soul prospers. III John 1:2

- ☐ Honor thy father and thy mother: that thy days may be long upon the land which the LORD thy God giveth thee, for this is the first commandment with promise. Exodus 20:12

- ☐ The days of our years are threescore years and ten; and if by reason of strength they be fourscore years, yet is their strength labour and sorrow; for it is soon cut off, and we fly away. Psalm 90:10

- ☐ Behold, happy is the man whom God corrects: therefore despise not thou the chastening of the Almighty; For he makes sore, and binds up: he wounds, and his hands make whole. Psalm 5:17-18

- ☐ And fear not them which kill the body, but are not able to kill the soul: but rather fear him which is able to destroy both soul and body in hell. Matthew 10:28

- ☐ In all this Job sinned not, nor charged God foolishly. Job 1:22

☐ But I have prayed for thee, that thy faith fail not: and when thou art converted, strengthen thy brethren. Luke 22:32

☐ For therein [in the gospel of Christ] is the righteousness of God revealed from faith to faith: as it is written, the just shall live by faith. Romans 1:17

*   *   *

My father fought a valiant battle against the ravages caused by infection from surgery.

He was a sportsman and a Tennessee Sports Hall of Fame Coach. Daily, I encouraged him in sports terminology . . . telling him, "We're still in the game." Or when there was progress, I would tell him, "It's only half-time and now we're up by two."

When my father died, I left his room, deflated.
At the time of his illness, one of my spiritual mentors was an associate pastor at his church. When I turned the corner after leaving the hospital suite, I saw her.

"We didn't win," I told her.

She said, "Oh, but we did." A Believer wins either way. If we are healed, we live on earth—we win. If we go to sleep in Jesus, we live again and we win. When we are in Christ, we are in a "Win-Win[6]."

Hallmarks of Humility

Hallmarks of Humility put us in touch with the suffering of our fellow man. It puts us in the exact position necessary for God to start to bless us with His healing power.

Consider these hallmarks of humility. Check the box next to the ones that resonate with you most.

☐ Humble yourselves therefore under the mighty hand of God that He may exalt you in due time. Casting all your care upon him; for he careth for you. I Peter 5: 6-7

☐ If my people, which are called by my name, shall humble themselves, and pray, and seek my face, and turn from their wicked ways; then will I hear from heaven, and will forgive their sin, and will heal their land.
II Chronicles 7:14

☐ For as the sufferings of Christ abound in us, so our consolation also aboundeth by Christ. II Corinthians 1:5

☐ And whosoever shall exalt himself shall be abased; and he that shall humble himself shall be exalted. Matthew 23:12

☐ But he giveth more grace. Wherefore he saith, God resisteth the proud, but giveth grace unto the humble. James 4:6

☐ And thou shalt remember all the way which the LORD thy God led thee these forty years in the wilderness, to humble thee, and to prove thee, to know what was in thine heart, whether thou wouldest keep his commandments, or no. Deuteronomy 8:2

Icons of Importunity

Importunity is our search for healing—to leave no stone unturned in the quest for wholeness. Read all you can. Pray for direction to be led into the pathways of those who can help you. Seek the Lord. Keep your heart merry by enjoying all the life you can (music, art, movement, laughter, reading, sports activities.)

Select the Bible promises that speak to your Importunity and petitions to God for healing.

- ☐ And shall not God avenge his own elect, which cry day and night unto Him, though He bear long with them? Luke 18:7

- ☐ Behold, the Lord's hand is not shortened, that it cannot save; neither his ear heavy, that it cannot hear: Isaiah 59:12

- ☐ And all things, whatsoever ye shall ask in prayer, believing, ye shall receive. Matthew 21:22

- ☐ If a son shall ask bread of any of you that is a father, will he give him a stone? Or if he ask a fish, will he for a fish give him a serpent? Or if he shall ask an egg, will he offer him a scorpion? If ye then, being evil, know how to give good gifts unto your children: how much more shall your heavenly Father give the Holy Spirit to them that ask him? Luke 11:11-13

- ☐ Behold, he that keepeth Israel shall neither slumber nor sleep. Psalm 121:4

- ☐ A merry heart doeth good like a medicine. Proverbs 17:22

There are two sides to the importunity lesson for us as Christians. When the requestor relentlessly begs for favor, the grantor must have the compassion of Christ and if possible, grant the request. Like Christ, we must be willing to look at our neighbor's condition and hear with our hearts, before we hear with our ears. We must fill some unspoken needs out of compassion, if we determine there is a need.

List the requests that you now have the power to fulfill in order to help someone in need.

_____

_____

_____

Opportunities for Obedience

Obedience is a responsibility, but it carries with it, a blessing. The blessing is the harmony that it fosters between man and his Creator. Which of these texts resonate most within you?

□   And in thy seed shall all the nations of the earth be blessed; because thou hast obeyed my voice. (Genesis 22:18)

□   If they obey and serve him, they shall spend their days in prosperity, and their years in pleasures.(Job 36:11)

□   And Samuel said, Hath the LORD as great delight in burnt offerings and sacrifices, as in obeying the voice of the LORD? Behold, to obey is better than sacrifice, and to hearken than the fat of rams. (I Samuel 15:22)

God has made provision for those of us who fall short of the mark and disobey. It is found in the following text:

□   And refused to obey, neither were mindful of thy wonders that thou didst among them; but hardened their necks, and in their rebellion appointed a captain to return to their bondage: but thou art a God ready to pardon, gracious and merciful, slow to anger, and of great kindness, and forsookest them not. (Nehemiah 9:17)

Milestones in Ministry

List three ways that you can use what you learned during your personal journey to help others.

1. _____
2. _____
3. _____

You can gain spiritual wisdom by studying the Word of God. Through the scriptures, God has given me answers to my problems over and over again. Each time that I am Spiritually led, I am pleased, yet somewhat amazed how He guides me in ways in which the 'world' does not believe, understand, or validate.

Think about a problem you may be facing. The problem can be physical, spiritual or emotional. Ask God to give you answers. As an act of faith, open the Bible to the location that God impresses upon you to read. While reading, you may become inspired to read from another book or chapter. Follow your inspiration. Keep reading until you understand your problem better.

When you have been healed, relieved of your burdens or enlightened, go on God's errands. Glorify Him in your walk, not only in your talk.

The five traits that lead to wellness are the same that lead to salvation: Faith, Humility, Importunity, Obedience, and Ministry. That is why Christ could both heal sickness and save souls, simultaneously.

Something Extra . . . .

What can you do while you are waiting for healing to occur?

Engage in Creative Healing
A Gallup Poll cited that 96% of all Americans believe in a Higher
Power or Universal Spirit. People who meditate, reflect daily,
and trust in God attest to the benefits of the spiritual alignment
that it brings. A walk on the beach, through the woods, on a
nature trail[5], or in your own backyard garden can bring peace
and repose. These activities can help you to strongly connect
with the Creator. In times of wellness, many people do not think
about God. But when sickness and despair fall upon human
beings, the natural response is to seek help from God.

In 2000, my mother had a knee replacement. As she reached
a new milestone during her physical therapy session, she
exclaimed, "Praise the Lord." The therapist remarked to her,
"People who know God have an easier time [recovering from]
with this surgery." During times of personal crisis, the belief that
you do not face your problems alone promotes resolution and
brings comfort. Even if you are not a Christian, you will benefit if
you spend some time everyday:

- Thinking about your life and its purpose
- Counting your blessings
- Reflecting over the day's events
- Writing your feelings in a journal
- Giving thanks
- Planning for personal time and activities that you enjoy

In addition to these traditional meditation activities, take
the challenge to medicate yourself through Creative Healing.
Creative Healing is the use of the arts: reading (biblio), music,
art, movement, and even laughter to promote wellbeing.

Participating in Creative Healing can provide an avenue for diversion.

Sports and Movement Therapy

Those who participate in sports find that movement allows the body to remain lithe and flexible over time[7]. Depending upon your fitness level and condition, select low-impact or high-impact activities. Walking is my favorite. On the island of Bermuda, there are some residents, well into their seventies and eighties, who enjoy a daily swim. Among their peers, these individuals demonstrate the most vitality, vigor, and stamina.

Like sports, aerobic exercises are cathartic and expressive.

Above all, select some type of activity that allows you to move your muscles and limbs.

Bibliotherapy

In a similar sense, reading books can provide a diversion from the life issues you may be facing. Recently I talked to a successful business manager. He recalled his high school experience to me as one that had been peppered with family troubles. These troubles were due to a parent who battled mental illness. The manager credited his own survival to a high school English teacher who provided for him books about far away places and exciting events. The books became the vehicle that provided solace and comfort for the young man. They rescued him from a shattered home environment. Reading caused the young man to be very well-read and educated beyond his formal education. It sparked his ambition to achieve. It kept him from becoming a victim of his environment. None of his classmates suspected the student's family difficulties. This was bibliotherapy at its best.

Like this young man, you too, may be facing tough issues. By selecting books with stimulating or interesting topics, you may be able to find a temporary solace. There is a strong possibility that you will return more invigorated, refreshed and thereby, better equipped to tackle your issues.

The clinical application of reading books for healing is called bibliotherapy. "Bibliotherapy", according to Jacqueline Stanley in Reading to Heal, "is the therapeutic use of books in the treatment of illnesses or personal problems" (p.3). She further states, "In Ancient Greece a plaque was placed over libraries stating: "A Place of Healing for the Soul" . . . and by 1850, every major mental hospital had a library" (p.4).

The benefits of bibliotherapy are many. In a personal crisis, reading subject-specific material can give you a proper understanding of the related social, emotional or spiritual issues. Through reading and processing your thoughts, you simulate a counseling relationship with the author. As the reader, you can gain awareness about the subject, acquire knowledge, experience attitudinal shifts and, ultimately, make behavior changes. As the reader, you obtain treatment at your own pace—whenever you need aid and comfort, the books are there. Your reading is personal; you can include others in your treatment or choose not to.

If you have a physical illness or medical condition, reading can also give you more information about your illness and help you to make informed decisions about your treatment and care. Once you are healed, reading can help you to maintain your wellness.

Music Therapy
Another form of creative healing is music therapy. We often hear the adage, "Music soothes the savage beast." You may recall the Biblical story of how David saved his own life from the hand of the crazed Saul by strumming his harp:

16 The spirit of the Lord left Saul and an evil spirit from God was upon Saul . . . . 23And it came to pass, when the evil spirit from God was upon Saul, that David took an harp and played it with his hand: so Saul was refreshed, and was well, and the evil spirit departed from him. (KJV)

The Biblical record states that King Saul put down the javelin and David was unharmed. (I Samuel 18:10)

I recall a similar personal healing experience with music, specifically, Chopin's Prelude in E minor. In the midst of a personal emotional, crisis, I played this work on piano. As I played it over and again, it seemed that the melody and its massaging harmonies bathed my emotions and soothed my restlessness like a cooling brook covers parched rocks after a long drought. The tension and release of the prelude's chromatic harmonies worked through my distress as skilled hands can manipulate throbbing muscles. Looking back over that experience, I marvel at what the Poet of the Piano (Frederic Chopin) was able to achieve through "25 measures and an anacrusis.[8]" I received healing. It was personal and effective. It was through music.

Department stores routinely use music therapy. After sampling factors such as their typical customer's age and economic/social status, merchants select and pipe in music that will motivate the customer to stay in the store longer. The longer they stay in the store, of course, the more they buy.

Laughter Therapy
Your brain receives a similar release when you laugh. Laughter therapy is the most newly documented form of creative healing. At this writing a few authors have written on the subject, conducted workshops, and consulted with organizations about how to use humor to reduce stress in the workplace. These writers say that laughter increases oxygen levels, releases endorphins from the brain cells, and strengthens the immune system. The strongest case for laughter therapy among other forms of creative healing is that laughter has an immediate effect on one's mood. It can break the chain of despair instantly. Other forms of creative healing are more process-oriented and if the user is not careful, the thoughts of despair can co-exist while the art form is being expressed, practiced, performed, or engaged in.

Art Therapy
Because an artist's canvas or other medium is a reflection of the mind's eye, participation in artistic activity can assist in a release of suppressed feelings or can allow an individual to express the content of the soul. Samuels and Lane (1998) reinforce this idea

in their book *Creative Healing*: "An artist is a way of being, a way of seeing. An artist looks at light, at shadows. An artist looks deeply into each moment (Ridley-Smith, 2001 quotes Samuels and Lane, 1998, p.107)."

With this in mind, consider the artistic imagery David conveyed in II Samuel 23:4 when he wrote:

He is like light flooding the earth at dawn on a cloudless day; He is like the sun that fills the sky after the rain; He makes every blade of grass sparkle like a diamond in the field and sprout from the ground. (The Clear Word).

Whether through art, laughter, music, movement, or reading, creative therapy can play a part in helping you to achieve and maintain a sense of personal balance and wellness. Use the following tips to explore creative therapy.

Tips:
- Visit a website on Laughter Therapy
- Visit the church, hall, or synagogue of your choice on a regular basis
- Unleash the artist inside you!
- Play a musical instrument, alone or in a group. If you do not play an instrument, compile a personal play list and listen to it regularly.
- Choose a mode of artistic expression. Make it a part of your schedule as you add more preferred activities to your schedule.
- Engage in the art form and journal about your results. Use the "Schedule and Reflect" form for your journaling. Request these forms at info@breakco.com.

Schedule

Required Activities   Date _____   **Preferred Activities**

_____   _____
_____   _____
_____   _____
_____   _____
_____   _____
_____   _____
_____   _____
_____   _____
_____   _____
_____   _____
_____   _____
_____   _____
_____   _____
_____   _____
_____   _____
_____   _____

Schedule

Create a road map for your day. Remember to schedule both required and preferred activities. Identify must-do activities with an asterisk.

Reflect ™

Required Activities	Date _____	Preferred Activities

Touching
Moments

Successes

Regrets

Funny
Stories

Feelings of
Inadequacy

Memorable
Events

Think About It:
Record today's data. Use the memory joggers in the margin to help you remember significant events of the day.

Keep Your Bubble Centered! © 1998

*   *   *

Creative Healing is good for:

Creating Psychological Distance between you and the problem
It is effective in providing relief for the types of problems that are usually resolved in time (grief, loss, anxiety). Creative Healing helps in these situations because it puts psychological distance between you and the problem. This has the same effect as 'time.'

Giving you a Temporary Diversion from your problem
Use Creative Healing to work on problems that are not life-threatening—when you are not in immediate danger. When you are endangered or when a loss of life or limb is at stake, a more immediate intervention is necessary. Don't be 'penny wise and pound foolish.'

Enabling you to enjoy the Balance of Your Life
From the moment we are born, we actually begin the process of dying. Disease, misfortune, and emotional issues can hasten and draw our attention to that process. Creative Healing can restore quality to your life and in doing so, you can begin living with your illness, rather than dying from it.

ENDNOTES

1   The evidence that Jesus practiced pharmacology is as follows:

When he had thus spoken, he spat on the ground, and made clay of
the spittle, and He anointed the eyes of the blind man with the clay,
And said unto him, Go, wash in the pool of Siloam. He went his way
therefore, and washed, and came seeing.
John 9:6

2   The Two Great Commandments, are these:

Jesus said unto him, Thou shalt love the Lord thy God with all thy
heart, and with all thy soul, and with all thy mind. This is the first
and great commandment. And the second is like unto it, Thou
shalt love thy neighbour as thyself. On these two commandments
hang all the law and the prophets.
Matthew 22: 37-40

3   Importunity is shameless persistence. This definition was given
by Joel Osteen on a Television Evangelistic program.

The Bible gives this example:

And he said unto them, Which of you shall have a friend, and shall
go unto him at midnight, and say unto him, Friend, lend me three
loaves; For a friend of mine in his journey is come to me, and I
have nothing to set before him? And he from within shall answer
and say, Trouble me not: the door is now shut, and my children are
with me in bed; I cannot rise and give thee. I say unto you, Though
he will not rise and give him, because he is his friend, yet because
of his importunity he will rise and give him as many as he needeth.

4   Obedience to God

After Christ had been crucified, buried, and had resurrected, Paul and the disciples continued to teach about Christ. They were imprisoned and brought before the high priest. When defending their practice to teach the multitudes about Christ, Paul and the other disciples echoed, "We ought to obey God rather than men."

5   Reverend Gwen Brown-Felder, June 13, 2003.

6   In this printing, sports was included to create the section on movement. It was contributed by Dr. Leslie Holder, based on his personal experience. As part of his own personal therapeutics, Leslie enjoys nature, particularly spending time on the beach (early morning), or in the woods and vigorous exercise such as swimming in the ocean and playing basketball (even past the age of 65).

7   The anacrusis in music is also called the "pick-up beat." The pick up beat occurs, in this case, at the beginning of a song or composition. It provides a rhythmic accent to the first beat of the first measure, making it sound stronger and more emphatic.

REFERENCES

Agatson, Arthur, M.D. 2003. *The South Beach Diet*. New York: Random House.

Blanco, Ph.D., Jack J. 1994. *The Clear Word: An Expanded Paraphrase of the Bible*. Hagerstown, MD: Review and Herald Publishers.

Bostick, Alan. 1999. (Sunday, July 25) "The Art of Healing: Vanderbilt Hospital treat patients with music, poetry and art." *The Tennessean*, page 1k.

Lockyear, Herbert. 1958. *All the Men of the Bible*. Grand Rapids: Zondervan.

Pearsall, Paul, Ph.D. 1987. *SuperImunnity: Master Your Emotions & Improve Your Health*. New York: McGraw-Hill.

Smith, Constance Ridley. 2001. *Keep Your Bubble Centered: How to Achieve Personal Balance*. Nashville: Breakthrough Communications.

Stanley, Jacqueline. 1999. *Reading to Heal: How to Use Bibliotherapy to Improve Your Life*. Boston: Element Books.

The Holy Bible Authorized King James Version (KJV), *Crown Reference Edition, 1985.* Nashville: Holman Bible Publishers.

Vine, W.E., Unger, Merrill F. and William White, Jr. 1985. *Vine's Expository Dictionary of the Bible*. Nashville: Thomas Nelson, Inc.

Online References:
Bibletab.com, Online Concordance
Containing one reference from the New American Bible

http://www.biblegateway.com
King James Version

Solution
(for Codebreaker Puzzle)

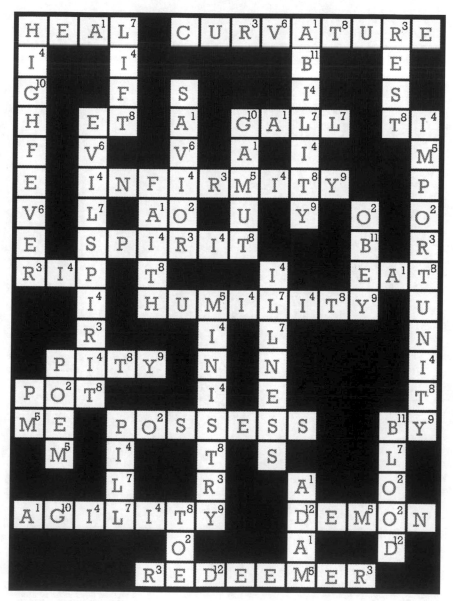

Hope

This chapter discusses biblical women of hope: those who mothered the kings of Judah in the lineage of Christ, the Messiah. Some mothers were good. Some were evil. This chapter will offer comparisons to the role of motherhood today so that today's women can appreciate the power of the mother's influence either for good or for evil. The opening story is about the birth of Pharez, a child whose birth symbolized the Hope of the Jewish nation, which was the birth of the Messiah. It also symbolizes hope and destiny fulfillment in the lives of mankind.

Although it appeared that his twin brother, Zarah, would be born first, Pharez had a destiny that could not be interrupted. Pharez "burst forth" to become the progenitor of the Messiah. Those who followed in the lineage of Christ also fulfilled their God-ordained destiny. The role of their mothers was key. These are the Women of Hope.

As today's women of hope, we can shape the destiny of our children as we:

- ☐ Make God first and serve Him only
- ☐ Become women of principle
- ☐ Cultivate the characteristics of a "good" woman

Women of Hope
Shape Destiny

Hope is both a noun and a verb. Hope, in its noun form, and faith have similar meanings[1], but they are not exactly the same.

Faith is a strong belief that is based on one's convictions. Faith can be somber, reverent, or joyous. Martyrs show strong faith even when they are about to die for a cause they believe in. For a Christian, faith is a look into the face of reality. It causes the believer to say, "whatever comes my way, good or bad, I believe God can handle it. I trust Him to work out what is best for me."

Hope is different. It is joyful anticipation. Hope looks forward to a pleasant outcome and a bright future. A good example of hope is the feeling that an expectant mother has when she is carrying a child in her womb.

With hope, the mother-to-be plans for and projects the best. She carefully selects items for the nursery and a name for the baby in the happy, joyful expectation that everything will be delightful. In this sense, hope stretches toward the ideal.

This chapter highlights women of hope and captures their spirit. Each woman who is discussed aspired to become the Vessel that God would choose to bring forth the awaited Messiah. Each carried, delivered, and mothered with this purpose in mind. Each enabled their sons to achieve their true potential.

Because of the Jewish custom, each mother probably recognized the power she would have as Queen Mother[2]. Many of them wielded power and influence while their sons reigned. The wicked ones like Maachah set up idols (I Kings 15:13).[3] Admirable ones like Mary, the mother of Jesus, wielded their influence for godly causes. One such godly cause was when Mary asked Jesus to turn the water into wine at the wedding feast in Cana of Galilee. Mary was keenly aware of His destiny and knew that Jesus had entered the world with a Divine Purpose.

Like these Mothers of Hope, I have also discovered that a child enters the world with a God-given purpose that only he or she can fulfill. Sometimes this purpose is foreshadowed at birth.

I recall an experience that happened to me while I was in the delivery room giving birth to my first child. During his examination, the young obstetrician informed me that my child was positioned face up, rather than face down. He communicated a plan to me that went as follows: "As the baby is coming out, Mrs. Smith, I'm going to ask you to stop pushing. At that time, I will turn the baby over so that she will be born face down as she should be."

The baby presented after another contraction or two. Then the young obstetrician commanded, "Stop pushing—I'm about to turn the baby." Tried, I did. But I soon discovered that there was a momentum which was greater than any plan that the young obstetrician had devised or that I could carry out. Baby Ashley burst forth with strength and purpose that no man could interrupt or delay.

A similar momentum occurred at the birth of Pharez, the first-born twin of Tamar and Judah. His story is recorded in Genesis 38. Genesis 38: 27-30 says:

> And it came to pass in the time of her travail, that, behold, twins were in her womb. And it came to pass, when she travailed, that the one put out his hand; and the midwife took and bound upon his hand a scarlet thread, saying, "This came out first." And it came to pass, as he drew back his hand, that, behold, his brother came out; and she said, How hast thou broken forth? This breach be upon thee: therefore his name was called Pharez. And afterward came out his brother, that had the scarlet thread upon his hand; and his name was called Zarah.

The Strong's Hebrew Lexicon says that 'breach' is the Hebrew word *"sabah"*, meaning to burst. Pharez "burst forth" to fulfill his destiny, which was to be the progenitor of the lineage of the Messiah.

Although it appeared that Zarah would be born first, Pharez had a destiny that could not be interrupted. Through the loins of Pharez, the promise of the Messiah was to be fulfilled. As the firstborn of Tamar and Judah, it was Pharez's loins that produced the lineage of David and of Jesus Christ. This was his purpose.

1 "The book of the generation of Jesus Christ, the son of David, the son of Abraham.
2 Abraham begat Isaac; and Isaac begat Jacob; and Jacob begat Judas and his brethren;
3 *And Judas begat Phares and Zara of Thamar; and Phares begat Esrom;* and Esrom begat Aram; [emphasis supplied]
4 And Aram begat Aminadab; and Aminadab begat Naasson; and Naasson begat Salmon;
5 And Salmon begat Booz of Rachab; and Booz begat Obed of Ruth; and Obed begat Jesse;
6 And Jesse begat David the king; and David the king begat Solomon of her that had been the wife of Urias;" (Matthew 1: 1-6)

This passage of scripture (Matthew 1:1-6) represents fourteen generations from Abraham to David.

Fourteen additional generations continue to trace Christ's lineage, from David's son, King Solomon, to King Jehoiakim, under whose reign Judah was captured by the Babylonians. Their stories are recorded in the Old Testament books of I Kings, II Kings, I Chronicles, II Chronicles, and Jeremiah.

And . . .

52

Generations from Abraham to the Birth of Jesus Christ

14 = Abraham to David

14 = Solomon to Jehoiakim

<u>14 =</u> Judah's exile to the birth of Christ
52

Fourteen final generations span the time from Judah's exile to the birth of Christ (read Matthew 1:12-16).

The stories of the Old Testament Kings (from Solomon to Jehoiakim) are dispersed throughout the Old Testament books of I Kings, II Kings, I Chronicles, II Chronicles, and Jeremiah. However, their names are succinctly listed in Matthew Chapter 1, beginning with verse 7. This is one example of how the Old Testament and the New Testament interpret and verify each other.

The Old Testament writers talked about these kings as they recorded the history of Israel and Judah and their conquests. But Matthew compiled his listing of the kings as a "who begat whom," perhaps for mothers. Matthew shows how God's purpose was accomplished, generation by generation, with each birth. For mothers, it reinforces the extreme honor which accompanies the birth of a child and the responsibility which accompanies the honor.

Like the mother of Samson, today's Mother of Hope will show concern for the development of her unborn child while it is in her womb. She will abstain from activities, foods, and substances that will be detrimental to her child's future well-being. After the birth of the child, she will provide an environment in which the child's God-given abilities and talents can thrive. She will recognize that there is also power in motherhood. A responsible, godly mother will use this power to accomplish good purposes. She will not use her power to accomplish evil purposes.

In summary, every child's life is an opportunity for achieving purpose, for literally bursting forth to achieve their destiny, in the manner that Pharez did. Every assignment to "mother" is a woman's opportunity to shape destiny. Good motherhood provides the environment and sets in place the conditions that are necessary for purpose achievement. Further, good motherhood anticipates or hopes for the most positive outcome.

Scriptures Support the Role of Motherhood

The prophet Malachi touched upon the importance of motherhood as he counseled the priests of Malachi 2 not to deal treacherously with the wives of their youth. For it is in motherhood and, ideally, in partnership with fatherhood, that a godly seed is raised up (Malachi 2:15).

Biblical mothers in the lineage of Christ knew the importance of their role. There was a professed expectation that God would send a Messiah. Each mother tended to her male offspring in expectation that she would have the distinct, godly honor of mothering the Messiah. The following table lists the Kings of Judah. It graphically portrays the lineage of Christ, who was called the Lion from the tribe of Judah.

The names of the kings who are considered to be in the lineage of Christ are marked with an asterisk.

Kings of Judah in the Lineage of Christ

*Only those kings whose names are marked with (*) are listed in the genealogy of Christ in Matthew 1: 7-13

Lineage of mother	Mother	Father	King	Age/ Years of their Reign	Evaluation
Eliam Ahithopel	Bathsheba	David	Solomon*	30/39 years	Good
Ammonitess	Naamah	Solomon	Rehoboam*	22 years	Evil
Daughter of Abishalom	Maachah	Rehoboam	Abijam*	3 years	Evil
Daughter of Abishalom	Maachah	Abijam	Asa*	38 years	Evil
Daughter of Shilhi	Azubah	Asa	Jehoshaphat*	35/25 years Co-reigned with son	Good
Daughter of Ahab; Lineage of Omri	Daughter of Ahab	Jehoshaphat	Jehoram*	32/8 years Co-reigned with father	Evil
King Ahab and Jezebel; granddaughter of Omri, King of Israel	Athaliah	Jehoram	Ahaziah	22/1 year	Evil
Ethbaal	Jezebel	King Ahab	Queen Mother Athaliah	6 years	Evil

Lineage of mother	Mother	Father	King	Age/ Years of their Reign	Evaluation
From the city of Beersheba	Zibiah	Ahaziah	Joash	7/40 years	Evil
From the city of Jerusalem	Jehoaddin	Joash	Amaziah	25/29 years	Good
From the city of Jerusalem	Jecoliah	Amaziah	Azariah* (Uzziah)	16/52 years	Good
Zadok	Jerusha	Azariah	Jotham*	25/16+4 years co-regent	Good
Unknown	Unknown	Jotham	Ahaz*	20/4 co-regent +12 years	Evil-offered his son as a burnt offering to Baal
Zechariah	Abijah	Ahaz	Hezekiah*	21/4+25 years	Best King
A woman in whom the Lord delighted 2 Kings 21:1	Hephzibah	Hezekiah	Manasseh*	12/55 years	Worst King
Haruz from the city of Jotbah	Meshullemeth	Amon	Amon*	22/2 years	Evil
Adaiah from the city of Bozkath	Jedidah	Amon	Josiah*	8/31 years	Good
From the city Beersheba	Zibiah	Ahaziah	Joash	7/40 years	Evil
From the city of Jerusalem	Jehoaddin	Joash	Amaziah	25/29 years	Good
From the city of Jerusalem	Jecoliah	Amaziah	Azariah* (Uzziah)	16/52 years	Good
Zadok	Jerusha	Azariah	Jotham*	25/16 years + 4 years co-regent	Good
Unknown	Unknown	Jotham	Ahaz*	20/4 co-regent + 12 years	Evil-offered his son as a burnt offering to Baal
Zechariah	Abijah	Ahaz	Hezekiah*	21/4+25 years	Best King
A woman in whom the Lord delighted 2 Kings 21:1	Hephzibah	Hezekiah	Manasseh*	12/55 years	Worst King
Haruz from the city of Jotbah	Meshullemeth	Amon	Amon*	22/2 years	Evil

Lineage of mother	Mother	Father	King	Age/ Years of their Reign	Evaluation
Adaiah from the city of Bozkath	Jedidah	Amon	Josiah*	8/31 years	Good
Jeremiah from the city of Libnah	Hamutal	Josiah	Jehoahaz	23/3 months	Evil
Pedaiah from the city of Rumah	Zebudah	Josiah	Eliakim* (Jehoiakim)	25/11 years	Evil (During this reign, Judah was taken into Babylonian captivity)
Elnathan from the city of Jerusalem	Nehushta	Jehoiakim	Jehoiachin	8/3 months	Evil
Jeremiah the city of Libnah	Hamutal	Josiah	Mattaniah (Zedekiah)	21/11 years	Evil (appointed by Nebuchadnezzar during captivity)
Grandson of Shaphan	Unknown	Ahikam	Gedaliah appointed governor by Nebuchad-nezzar	Set up by Nebuchadnezzar; Ruled 2 months, the slain by Nethaniah, father of Ismael	

Note: In the lineage of Christ, there were fourteen generations from Abraham to King David; fourteen from King Solomon until Judah was taken into exile by Babylonian King Nebuchadnezzar and again, fourteen generations from their captivity until the birth of Christ (Matthew 1:17). This makes 52 generations from Abraham to Jesus Christ.

Incidentally, this tribe of Judah that is mentioned was the same Judah who begat Pharez. From Judah to Pharez, then to David, the King who begat Solomon. This table picks up from the ending of the begats of Matthew 1:1-6. It starts with Solomon (verse 7) and ends with Eliakim (verse 13).

Scripture Classifies Kings Good or Evil

The Bible classifies the kings according to their practices and obedience to God's law. They were deemed to be good if they adhered to the Law, tore down idols, put God first, and built altars to God. They were considered to be evil if they practiced idolatry. This included building high places and altars to strange gods and offering sacrifices—even their own children—to these strange gods.

The table shows that it was indeed possible for a father and son to be classified on the opposite ends of the spectrum. The adage, "Like father, like son" did not always hold true in the case of these kings. For example, Good King Jehoshaphat was followed by his son, Jehoram, who was considered to be evil. Father Hezekiah was cited to be the best King while his son Manasseh was cited to be the worst of all.

There is a strong suggestion that the mother's influence was also a determining factor. The Bible is consistent in giving the lineage of each king. I expected to find the father's name listed. After all, I have always regarded the Bible as a patriarchal recollection. However, it was fascinating to me to find that the Bible also recorded who the mother was in each case, except for one: the mother of evil King Ahaz.

In the following sections, we will learn how the Bible characterizes the kings of Judah <u>and</u> their mothers.

3 I's of Evil

➢ Idolatry
➢ Incest
➢ Influence

The Power of an Evil Influence: Evil Kings

The Bible classifies many kings as having been evil. Evil kings were characterized by their ties to ungodly practices such as idolatry and incest. In addition, the influence of their evil mothers was also a factor in the development of their evil characteristics.

Several evil kings had evil mothers, beginning with one of Solomon's ungodly wives, Naamah, the Ammonitess, who bore for him the evil King Rehoboam. The Ammonites, you may remember, were the people who descended from the incestuous sexual relationship that Lot had with his youngest daughter after Sodom and Gomorrah had burned to the ground.

Two other evil kings, Jehoram and Ahaziah, were descendents of evil King Ahab who, among other flaws, was an idolater. In fact, both King Ahab and his father King Omni were idolaters and Kings of *Israel*, not Judah. Ahab's wife Jezebel was a Baal worshipper. Her father's name was Ethbaal. Jehoram was the son of the good king, Jehoshaphat, who did a lot to restore the spirituality and the economic storehouses of Judah. However, Jehoshaphat intermarried with the daughter of King Omni and his son Jehoram was a product of the mother (Davidiy, accessed online 2008, p. 2). The Bible classified Jehoram as a good king for the first few years when he co-reigned with his father, King Jehoshaphat. But for the following eight years of Jehoram's reign, he was considered to be an evil king.

II Kings 8:18 also records Jehoram as an evil king because of the influence of his wife Athaliah, the daughter of King Ahab and Jezebel, who caused him to "walk in the ways of the house of Ahab. If our supposition that Jehoram's mother was a daughter of King Omni is true, then Jehoram had a double influence for evil—first his mother, then his wife, Athaliah.

> "And he walked in the way of the kings of Israel, like as did the house of Ahab: for he had the daughter of Ahab to wife and he wrought that which was evil in the eyes of the Lord". (II Chronicles 21:6)

Jehoram's son, Ahaziah, reigned one year. He was considered evil. It was not a mere coincidence that Jezebel was his grandmother and Athaliah was his mother. After her son's death, Athaliah tried to destroy all of her grandchildren so that *she* could sit on the throne as Queen. Her reign is also considered to be an evil one.

Evil mothers provide examples which formulate their children's daily experiences. These early experiences are likely to shape their opinions, habits, and judgment in the future.

It is interesting to note that during the reigns wherein the kings were the genetic product of two parents who were considered to be evil, the kings are classified as evil. Their names are omitted from Matthew's listing of kings in the lineage of Christ. Consider the following:

Jehoram had one evil parent, named in the Bible as "the Daughter of King Ahab". Jehoram is listed among kings in the lineage of Christ. However, Jehoram married further into an evil lineage by taking Athaliah as his wife. Their son Ahaziah is not listed in the lineage, nor is Athaliah, who succeeded her son on the throne. Athaliah's grandson, Joash, and her great grandson, Amaziah, make the third and fourth generations[4] that were not considered to be in the lineage of Christ through Pharez who burst forth and, through his descendant, David, who became king.

This occurrence was foreshadowed in the second of the Ten Commandments that God gave to Moses on Mount Sinai. It is not a mere coincidence that the second commandment is based on the caution against practicing idolatry and that idolatry was also the legacy of King Ahab and Jezebel:

> 3 Thou shalt have no other gods before me . . . . 4 Thou shalt not make unto thee any graven image . . . . 5 Thou shalt not bow down thyself to them nor serve them: for I the Lord thy God am a jealous God, visiting the iniquity of the fathers unto the 3rd and 4th generation of them that hate me and showing mercy unto thousands of them that love me and keep my commandments. Exodus 20:3-6.

The next table outlines the four kings whose names were left out of Matthew's listing of 'who begat whom.' It shows those four kings were related to Jezebel.

To the 3rd and 4th Generations
of them that hate me . . .

King	Parents	Relationship to Jezebel	Commentary
Athaliah	Ahab and Jezebel	Jezebel's daughter, likely; but certainly Ahab's daughter & Omni's granddaughter	Proclaimed herself as Queen Mother after her son King Ahaziah died; she ordered all of his descendants to be killed. II Chronicles 22:10
Ahaziah	Jehoram and Athaliah	Jezebel's Grandson	He also walked in the ways of Israel, for his mother was his counselor to do wickedly. Wherefore he did evil in the sight of the Lord like the house of Ahab; for they were his counselors, after the death of his father to his destruction. II Chronicles 22:3-4
Joash	Ahaziah and Zibiah	Jezebel's Great Grandson	He did right in the sight of the Lord all the days of Jehoiada the priest, but slew his cousin Zedekiah after Priest Jehoiada's death. II Chronicles 23:22
Amaziah	Joash and Je- hoaddan	Jezebel's Great-Great Grandson	He did what was right in the sight of the Lord, but not with a perfect heart. II Chronicles 25:2

Note: Interestingly, the Kings who were descendants of the wicked Jezebel and King Ahab are omitted from Matthew's listing in the geneaology of Christ (see Matthew1: 7-11.)

The most documented evil King of Judah was King Ahaz. Ahaz was also a Baal worshipper. It was under his reign that Israel took Judah into captivity. This was a decisive victory for Israel, but because of Israel's unworthiness the Judeans were let go. Later, the Edomites and Philistines also took Judah into captivity (II Chronicles 28:17). Ahaz then appealed to the Assyrians for help, giving them the gold items in the temple as payment. In a time of challenge, Ahaz relied upon methods he had seen work for the heathens. He began to burn offerings and offer sacrifices to idols. He even offered his son as a burnt offering to Baal. In II Chronicles 28:19, the Bible records,

> "For God brought Judah low because of Ahaz."

Perhaps God did not list his mother's name in an act of mercy—to spare her embarrassment and to avoid shaming the family lineage. Perhaps Ahaz's was also in Jezebel's lineage (due to his Baal worship).

Again refer to the charts in this chapter as you ponder these details.

The Power of a Godly Influence:
Good Kings and Good Men of the Bible

The legacy created by the evil queen mothers is quite sobering. It reinforces the importance for mothers to be godly and to walk in harmony with God's word. When she is godly, a mother is better able to assist a child in living up to his or her God-given potential.

There is no guarantee that the child who is raised by a godly mother will always walk a path that is circumspect, but by her daily example, the child gains a template for godliness. Again, these patterns become guide posts for the child's actions, habits, and future decision-making.

Consider Mrs. Manoah and Hannah, mothers of Samson and Samuel. Both mothers cherished their roles. Hannah petitioned God to bless her womb before Samuel was born. So grateful was Hannah that God had allowed her to become a mother that she 'gave her son back to the Lord' to be trained in the priesthood under the tutelage of Eli. While he was not a king, Samuel became a man of God and played a key role in the lineage of the Messiah. He was the one that God selected to anoint David to be King of Israel, even while David was still a young shepherd boy.

Mrs. Manoah excelled at prenatal care. She did not drink wine while she carried Samson. While he was young, she instructed him in the Nazarite creed. Even as Samson attained the age to select for himself a wife, she and Samson's father continued to provide counsel and cautioned his selection of women who were outside of their faith. They raised him as well as any God-fearing parents could. But Samson did not heed their counsel. We are quite familiar with his demise (with Delilah) and the shameful way that he lost his strength, his eyesight, and his dignity. However, the Bible indicates that even as he died between the two pillars, his heart was repentant towards the teachings he had been given in his early life. In the end, his death was victorious in ways that his life could have been.

> "So the dead which he slew at his death were more than they which he slew in his life." Judges 16:30

Finally, there is the mother of King Manasseh, who reigned for 55 years. In II Kings 21:1, the Bible states that Manasseh's mother, Hephzibah, was a woman in whom the Lord delighted. His father was Hezekiah, whom the Bible describes as the Best King of Israel. Both of Manasseh's parents were godly, but the Bible tells us that Manasseh was the worst King of Israel. He built up altars for Baalim, practiced witchcraft, and sought familiar spirits and wizards. As much as his father Hezekiah did to turn from the ways of his father Ahaz and rid Israel of idolatry, Manasseh did not follow suit. Manasseh rebuilt idolatry. He provoked God to anger.

Manasseh's parents were perhaps as good as any could have been. What went wrong? The truth about Manasseh and his parents, Hephzibah and Hezekiah, can be our comfort when we have followed God's course and things go wrong despite our efforts.

That truth is that God has created man higher than any other being, in that man has free choice, the ability to reason, and the capability to make rational decisions. Inherent in this ability is the propensity also to make mistakes. Mercifully laid at the beginning of man's history, however, was God's plan to restore man to Himself so that man's mistakes would not separate him eternally from the Love of God.

The Bible tells us that later, after being sanctioned by God, Manasseh repented and tried to rectify some of the mistakes he had made, but his son Amon had inherited father Manasseh's tendency toward evil. Amon was judged to be an evil king. It wasn't until the next generation, that godliness was restored. Manasseh's grandson, Josiah, was considered to be a good king.

God is praised when mothers—and fathers—walk in obedience. They are blessed; the fruit of their womb flourishes. Read Deuteronomy 7: 9-21. Their children may walk through periods of darkness, but they should remain hopeful as they claim the Bible promise,

> "Train up a child in the way he should go, and when he
> is old, he should not depart from it." Proverbs 22:6

Think About It 💬

If idolatry was such a big infraction in Bible times, is it still a big infraction today?

Of course, it is not our practice to make golden calves and offer our children as burnt sacrifices. What does modern-day idolatry look like?

_____
_____
_____
_____
_____

1. What are the characteristics of a good mother?

_____
_____
_____
_____
_____

2. "How can you determine if you are walking as God would have you to walk?"

List 3-5 practices you would expect to see of a mother who is walking with God:

_____
_____
_____
_____
_____

These questions often arise—

a. Can a good mother produce a bad child?

b. Can good parents have evil children?

The term "good" is subjective. It may not mean the same thing to us that it means to God—as quoted in the Bible.

Some mothers have said "I'm a good mother . . . .

☐ I provide for my children. I buy them whatever they need."

☐ I'm a good mother, I'm not afraid to spank her when she needs it."

☐ They never had to want for food on the table or a place to sleep."

☐ I worked 3 jobs for my children so they could have things and wouldn't go without."

But how does the Bible define "good"?

Read Proverbs 31:10-31

By examining the women that God called good, what are the traits God is looking for in a Good Mother?

3. Do you believe in the concept of generational curses? Why or why not?

_____

_____

4. Do you believe in the concept of generational blessings and gifts? Why or why not?

_____

_____

5. Is there a relationship between what a child does and the characteristics of their parents and/or household of origin?

_____

_____

6. Is it possible for good parents to raise children who do evil deeds? Give examples to support your answer.

_____

_____

7. Is it possible for evil parents to raise children who do good deeds? Give examples to support your answer.

_____

_____

8. What advice can you give a couple who is expecting their first child?

_____

_____

_____

Consider the effect that a troubled home has on the well-being and disposition of a child. Is it possible that Adam and Eve's fall and necessity to relocate outside of Eden affected the climate of their relationship and household? Blame, loss, shame, and accusations may have caused the couple to share miserable times.

If so, they are not unlike modern couples who are facing marital challenges caused by life decisions and the pressures of life.

9. Is there a relationship between a troubled marriage and troubled children?

_____

_____

Hope Thrives Best when coupled with Principled Behaviors

Hope has its greatest effect when it is coupled with principled behaviors. Only when accompanied by principled behaviors will hope foster true joy. Hope does not facilitate, condone, or support wrong doing. The following case stories, two modern and a few Biblical ones, will show the ill effects of women whose hope was skewed by ambition, greed, and wrong doing.

Case Studies

In a major metropolitan city in the United States, a 17-year-old male who lived with his mother was arrested near his home for possession of drugs with the intent to resell. A raid of the home uncovered large sums of cash, drugs, and paraphernalia. The next morning, the local newspaper quoted the mother as saying, "He's such a good boy; I didn't know he was selling drugs." Similarly, two youth were building a bomb in the garage of one of their homes. The youths detonated the bomb at their high school and killed teachers and fellow students. Reports stated their parents were unaware of the bomb-building project in their garage.

It is the parents' and, specifically, the mother's responsibility to know what's going on under her tent and courageously face tough issues to rid her household of the accursed thing. A Christian mother orders the household based on certain unwavering principles based on "thus saith the Lord." She communicates them by her behaviour rather than relying solely on her spoken word.

As a teacher, I was always perplexed about students who didn't do homework. I once asked my own mother, "Momma, how did you convey to your own children that they should come home and do their homework everyday after school. I don't remember you telling us to do it. She replied, "I didn't have to tell you what to do. I lived it." This corresponds to the counsel to let the unbelieving husband be won by the conversation of their wives. (I Peter 3:1-7) In the Greek, the word, conversation, is not talk, it is deportment, conduct, or actions.

When something is wrong on the home front, the worst position for a woman to take is to abdicate responsibility and look the other way. This is unprincipled, non-assertive behavior. Non-assertiveness lets things happen; the chips fall where they may. A principled and assertive mother will address the issue and explain why it is a situation that violates the principles. She will begin to invite the other party to problem-solve and generate solutions to the uncomfortable situation. In extreme cases, those situations that pose violation to the Ten Commandment Law, the laws of the land, or will possibly cause the loss of life, there is no time to problem-solve. There is no need for diplomacy. The accursed thing must be gotten rid of immediately. This is assertive, principled behavior. Many women compromise principle and go along with dishonest schemes. They look the other way and scoot important issues "under the rug."

Such was the case, literally, with Achan Carmi of Zerah. Under the rug of his tent, lay articles of treason against God. This example of dishonesty was recorded in the Book of Joshua in the Old Testament, repeated in Acts 5 in the New Testament, and continues in the homes of modern women today. Let's examine what happened when people of the Bible allowed ungodly actions to exist in their households, without lifting up or living up to the standard.

Achan's Wife
Confident after the successful battle of Jericho, Joshua sent men to spy and stake out the city of Ai. After a favorable report, Joshua commanded a small troop to take this city. A brief skirmish left 36 Israelite casualties and a confused general. Petitioning to the Lord, Joshua found that the Lord was displeased with them because someone in the camp had taken spoils from Jericho although they had been instructed in Joshua 6:18-19, as follows:

> 18 . . . . And ye, in anywise keep your selves from the accursed thing, lest you make your selves accursed,

when you take up the accursed thing, and make the
camp of Israel a curse and trouble it.

19 . . . . But all the silver and gold, and vessels of brass
and iron, are consecrated unto the Lord: they shall
come into the treasury of the Lord.

Joshua called each of the tribes together to explain what the Lord
had shown him. By family, by household, and then by man, Joshua
examined them all. Finally, Achan confessed in Joshua 7:21:

"When I saw among the spoils a goodly Babylonish
garment, and 200 shekels of silver, and a wedge of
gold of 50 shekels weight, then I coveted them, and
took them, and behold they are hid in the earth, and
the silver under it."

For this act, the Bible records, the household of Achan was stoned
and all the possessions that he had, including his tent, were
burned. Although the Bible does not record anything specifically
about Achan's wife, or that he even had a wife, it is plausible
to deduce that because he had a tent, sons and daughters and
cattle (v. 24), that he also may have had a wife. The description of
Achan's household in Joshua 7: 24 compares with the description
of a household given in the Ten Commandments (Exodus 20:17).
If Exodus 20:17 can be considered as a template for Biblical
households, we can deduce that Achan also had a wife.

If this deduction is true, then it is hard to believe that Achan's
wife did not know about the articles hidden in the midst of
her 'living room.' For her alleged part in going along with her
husband's scheme, the whole household perished.

Rachel

A similar theme is found in the Bible story of Jacob's departure
from his uncle Laban's estate. When Jacob's caravan left, his
beloved wife Rachel stole some images from her father, Laban.
Laban pursued Jacob's caravan for seven days and searched the

contents of every tent. However, Rachel pretended that she was on her monthly period and couldn't stand up to be searched. Laban departed without searching underneath his daughter (Genesis 31:34-35) and therefore, without finding the hidden images.

Although Jacob was not aware of what his wife had done, Rachel had continued the legacy of trickery that started with Jacob's mother, Rebekah, and her brother Laban.

You may recall that with his mother Rebekah's help, Jacob tricked his father (Isaac) and his brother (Esau) out of the birthright. In turn, Jacob's uncle Laban tricked him into working an extra seven years for Rachel's hand in marriage. Rachel then tricked her father, Laban, regarding the stolen images. Later, Jacob and Rachel's precious son, Joseph, was victimized in a cruel scheme by which his brothers tricked Jacob into thinking that Joseph had been killed. My mother recited to me this precious rhyme when I was a child: "O what tangled webs we weave, when first we practice to deceive.[5]" Never was this poetic verse more true than in reference to the lineage of Jacob due to his mother Rebekah's influence.

<u>Sapphira</u>
There are times when the woman does not engineer the trickery, but takes part in carrying it out. This is what happened in the Bible story written in Acts Chapter 5 with a married couple, Ananais and Sapphira. The couple sold a possession with the intent to bless the ministry of the apostles. When they received more from it than they had anticipated, they withheld part of the proceeds. They stated the price lower than what they actually obtained for it. The apostle Peter confronted Ananais about this. Ananais fell dead. Three hours later, Sapphira appeared. Peter gave her a chance to answer for herself, lift up the standard and, perhaps, preserve herself and her household. He asked her in Acts 5:8:

> "Tell me whether you sold the land for so much? And
> she said yes for so much."

Sapphira had the opportunity to correct the record. She failed the opportunity.

Peter concluded the conversation by asking her in verse 9, "How is it that you have agreed together to tempt the Spirit of the Lord?"

In verse 10, the Bible records that Sapphira also fell dead.

Peter's second question to Sapphira is a warning to all of us who know what is right, but choose to go along with what is wrong, in hope that because God is in control, things will somehow work out for right.

Sarai

Perhaps this is the thinking that Sarai, wife of Abraham, demonstrated when she corroborated her husband's story: that she was his sister, rather than his wife (Genesis 12). In not wanting to anger King Abimelech, the pair almost caused a curse to fall upon themselves.

No matter how persuasive, charming, charismatic or, on the other hand, how forceful and intimidating the other person may be, to side with wrong in hope that the right thing will somehow work itself out is also wrong. Acts 5:9 calls this tempting the Spirit of the Lord.

This does not mean that the Holy Spirit is tempted to sin as we are. There is no 'sin calling' in the Holy Spirit. Instead, the word tempt in this case is more likely, "ekpeirazo". Ekpeirazo is similar to peirazo, which means to prove, typically in a good way. Vine's Expository Dictionary also explains that ekpeirazo is much stronger than peirazo, and that it probably means to challenge.

Ekpeirazo is the word that was used by Jesus to answer Satan in Matthew 4:7 and Luke 4:12 when Satan said to Jesus, "Go ahead, cast yourself down from this precipice. After all, isn't it written that the angels have been given charge of thee, to keep thee?" Jesus replied to Satan, the enemy, "Thou shalt not tempt (ekpeirazo) the Lord thy God." In other words, don't challenge God. Don't frustrate God's grace and mercy and require Him to perform a miraculous act to counterbalance wrong doing or presumption on your part.

In Sarah's case, she tempted or challenged God by her lack of courage and her unwillingness to boldly confront issues. By His example in the wilderness temptation, Christ has shown us what to do. Do what you know is right. Dare to challenge the enemy; lift up the standard in your household.

Consider this scenario:

Two college students were dating. The female student had a car. She confided in me, "My boyfriend asked me to drive my car by a local apartment complex while he and his friend went upstairs to "rip-off" a stereo set. He acted as if it were the most normal thing in the world to do on a Saturday night . . .

After being convicted for assisted burglary, she asked, "What was I thinking? I knew deep down that it was wrong. But he was so convincing that it was alright."

Achan, Rachel, Sapphira, Sarai and the modern women cited at the onset of this section failed. On some occasions, I have failed. Judas also failed. One Bible scholar[6] concluded that Judas did not expect that Christ would allow Himself to be crucified. He thought Christ would save Himself. He thought his actions would catapult Jesus to assume the leadership of an earthly Kingdom. It is not enough to feign ignorance and let things occur in your midst. Lift up the standard. For Jesus said, "and I, if I be lifted up will draw all men unto me."

<u>Vashti</u>

Lift up the standard and let God fight the battle. That is the message Queen Vashti taught us. Without the promise of success on the other side, Vashti departed from her husband's kingdom. She boldly refused to compromise her values and walked away from what we believe was an unreasonable demand. Like Vashti, when a wife makes a stand, she must be prepared to go the distance, if necessary. Although she may be right, she may also be afraid. She may have nowhere to go. Like the children of Israel, leaving sure bread and water in Egypt for freedom was good in principle, but it made their journey uncertain.

The Bible is purposefully, yet curiously, silent about how Vashti fared after leaving the King. If we deduce that King Ahasuerus' wine-induced request was for her to present herself immodestly, we can applaud Vashti for doing what was right, come what may.

Vashti's course is the one I used in similar matters of principle. At the time of this writing, I was battling at least two demons in my tent. I prayed to the Lord and asked Him to guide me. I lifted up His standard and asked Him whether I was wrong or right in my thinking. I asked Him to lead me—that I did not want to make a mistake. Then, in despair, I told Him, "it's too big for me to handle. I don't know how to begin to fix these issues. There is so much I just don't understand about it so Lord, you handle it." A great relief came over me as I gave these problems to God. As time went on, the problem still existed, yet, I doggedly continued to do what He had placed within my Spirit to do; what I believed to be my calling. In spite of many moments of despair, I agonizingly tried to do His will on earth. God built a hedge around me. He blessed me in spite of the mess. He gave me the desires of my heart. This walk of faith with God calmed my Spirit. I had a peace that passed all understanding. He made a way for my escape. He made me the head and not the tail. He didn't use my methods. He used His own. When God began to move on my behalf, I clearly knew that it was not me. The miracles that happened in my life were things that only a Sovereign God could do. He enlarged my territory and my influence for His name's sake. He prepared a table for me in the presence of my enemies.

Thanks be to God. I have seen the Lord's Hand of grace and mercy take control of a bad situation and work things out. I give God glory, praise, and honour for His work in my life.

I ask Him to continue to help my children to grow to achieve their God-given purpose. This is my hope. This is also my hope for you.

Points for Principled Behavior in Tough Times

1. Identify what is right. Use the Word of God to separate what is right from what is not right.

2. Say what you see
   State what you want
   Seek a mutual resolution

3. Don't waiver. Lift up the standard.

4. Above all, be kind in your words. Soften the delivery of your message so that your true intent won't be lost behind angry, explosive words that you can't take back.

Choose one of the Biblical Women that were discussed. Tell how she might have used steps 1-4 above to demonstrate principled behaviour in difficult times.

Encourage someone today:
Share a time when you lifted up a standard and God intervened on your behalf.

BIBLE PROMISE FOR YOU

When the enemy shall come in like a flood, the Spirit of the Lord will lift up a standard against it.

Isaiah 59:19

SOLVE THIS CLUES to reveal the names of Biblical women. Write each woman's name in the designated spaces on the puzzle.

DOWN
1 This woman joined her husband's scheme to cheat the apostles out of money they promised to give from the sale of their property.
2. This woman joined her husband's half-truth to King Abimelech, that she was his sister. (She was half-sister, but was also his wife).
3. This woman stole some images from her father Laban and sat on them so that he could not find them during his search of their tent.

ACROSS
4. This household was stoned because the man stole articles such as a Babylonish garment, silver, and gold from the battle of Jericho and hid them in the floor of his tent
5. This Queen refused to display herself in front of her husband's guests and was banished from the Kingdom.

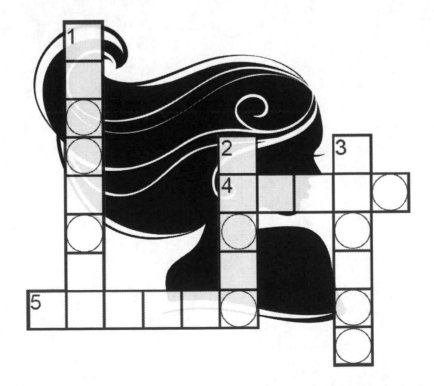

Circled Letter Puzzle

Each row and column in the puzzle contains circled letters. For example, in Column 1, there are three circled letters. Copy the circled letters into the circles below. Continue this process for each row and column, 1-5.

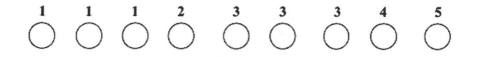

Now, unscramble the circled letters to reveal a word. This word is the characteristic that women and mothers must display. When coupled with hope, this word will bring favor to your household and harmony with God's plan for your life.

Write the unscrambled word in the blanks below.

____ ____ ____ ____ ____ ____ ____ ____ ____

Puzzle Solution on Page 92

Hope is Relevant for Motherhood Today

In the 1970's, Frank Klassen wrote a very useful study reference entitled, "The Chronology of the Bible." In the preface Klassen, wrote:

> "The lineage to Christ faced extinction continually, but in each generation, God intervened to preserve the Royal Seed . . . . the mothers involved knew their responsibility. Eve recognized the godly Seth . . . For God, said she, hath appointed me another seed instead of Abel (Genesis 4:25; 5:3); Sarah, at age 90, delighted in the birth of Isaac, for he was the fruit of the promise (Genesis 17:17, 21:5); Tamar was willing to give her life to preserve the seed of Judah (Genesis 38). Ruth was to be like Rachel and like Leah, which two did build the house of Israel (Ruth 4:11) . . . . and Mary said to the angel, "Behold the handmaid of the Lord; be it unto me according to that word (Luke 1:38.)" [paraphrase]

While reading the Klassen text, the Spirit suggested to me that each mother was equipped to do her part in preserving the Royal Seed. Each mother today is also equipped to handle the child that is on loan to her from God. She must accept the Providence and Provision of God as Eve did; she must wait on the Lord as Sarah learned to do. She must be willing to sacrifice to preserve the seed as Tamar was; and she must submit to the Lord's will as the Virgin Mary did. Looking at these mothers, we should be able to distill some distinct qualities that good mothers share.

Characteristics of a Good Mother

Over the past 22 years of motherhood, I've found that mothering is not an exact science. The fact is, being a mother is often a thankless job. Mothers often have to do the 'unpopular stuff'. They must manage: plan the meals; organize the troops for efficiency and productivity; lead by example, whether they want to, or not; and control those occurrences that do not meet the family standard. In all this, a mother must love and show tenderness. She must also be submissive to her husband's leadership, be supportive and work alongside him. A mother is a manager of the hearts within the home and the resources that support It.

As a teenager who had all the answers, I actually thought my mother's policies and practices were borderline ridiculous. At age 14 I made a list of all the things I would never do, if and when I became a mother. A few years ago, I found that list. I laughed to myself when I realized that I do all the things I swore that I never would. And I am proud to say that I do.

Now that I am the mother of a teenage daughter about the same age, I have a deeper appreciation of the philosophy that my mother employed to raise me and the challenges she faced. I realize what it takes to be a good mother—some of which I am and some of which I wish I were more of.

A good mother is not confused by things that are ungodly. In order to exert the proper influence for good, she must put God first. In essence, she must not engage in modern-day idolatry. She must not entertain any ideas or allow any practices to enter the home that are contrary to God's will.

A good mother is:

> Full of Hope
> Loving
> Consistent
> Firm
> Dependable
> Organized
> Supportive, and
> Leads by Example

All of those things my mother was. What's more, she was a woman of God.

Several years before she died, I took the opportunity to thank my mother for the years of unwanted piano lessons, strict rules, and conducting background checks on my friends and associates. In the years that followed, she often cited my "Thank you Mom, for Everything" to her friends. I'm glad I gave her those flowers while she lived.

If you have a mother alive today, why not give a bouquet while she can bask in its fragrance?

If you are a mother and are becoming weary in doing well, press on in your faith work. [S]he who is faithful to the end, God will give a crown of life (Revelation 2:27).

After my mother died, I found a handwritten scripture in her study basket. I include it now as a Bible Promise For You.

BIBLE PROMISES FOR YOU

"Thy mother is like a vine in thy blood, planted by the waters: she was fruitful and full of branches by reason of many waters."

Ezekiel 19:10

There is Hope for the Hopeless....

TEST YOUR KNOWLEDGE - SOLVE THE FOLLOWING CLUES ABOUT A FAMILY WHO WAS TORN BY DECEIT

Across

1 A form of dishonesty based on deception
3 Employed his nephew for 14 years to pay off a 7-year commitment
4 Tricked out of his birthright
5 Oldest daughter who became part of the dowry scheme against Jacob
7 Saw the ladder of God's promise in his dream
9 The place where Abraham and Sarai lived long before the birth of Isaac; also the name of one of Abraham's brothers (Genesis 11:31)
13 Garment that caused jealousy among brothers

Down

2 Mother who devised a scheme to bless her favorite son
3 Jacob built an altar in this city and renamed in Bethel (Genesis 28:19)
6 Laban was called the son of _____(Genesis 24:15)
8 Son of Jacob and Rachel who was sold into slavery by his brothers
10 Blind father who mistakenly blessed the youngest son instead the eldest
12 The first three letters of the city from which Essau took a wife
13 God told Laban in a dream, "Take heed that thou not speak to Jacob good or __."
14 Deceit comes to no good_____.

Crossword

Solution on page 98

1T	2R	I	C	K	E	4R	Y		8J		
	E					A		13C	O	A	T
3L A	B	A	6N			C			S		
U	4E	S	A	U		H			E		10I
Z	K		H			E			P		S
	5J	A	12C	O	13B	5L	10E	A	H		A
	9H	A	R	A	N		N				A
		N		D		D					C

Crossword Solution *(page 99)*

SOLUTIONS *(pages 88-89)*

DOWN

    1   SAPPHIRA

    2   SARAI

    3   RACHEL

ACROSS

    4   ACHAN

    5   VASHTI

Circled Letters: P P I R C E L N I

Unscrambled Word: P R I N C I P L E

Something Extra . . . .

With the Spirit of Pharez:
Burst into Your Purpose

I believe that every human being enters the world with a God-given purpose that only he or she can fulfill. Sometimes this purpose is foreshadowed at birth.

Although it appeared that his twin brother, Zarah would be born first, Pharez had a destiny that could not be interrupted. Through the loins of Pharez, the promise of the Messiah was fulfilled. As the firstborn of Tamar and Judah, it was Pharez's loins that produced the lineage of David, and of Jesus Christ. This was his purpose.

Pharez and the others who followed in the lineage of Christ, lived the destiny God ordained for them.

How can we, like Pharez, follow God's plan for our lives? The key can be found in the acronym, A-S-S-E-R-T.

Pray for direction. Ask God to help you to ASSERT yourself in this area. Here's what is meant by ASSERT:

Assess your gifts and abilities.

- Make an inventory of what you do best.
  _____

  _____

- Ask yourself, "What's in my hands?" "What abilities do I have?"
- Think back to your earliest memory of play or activity,
  o   What was the first toy you enjoyed? _____

o   What was the first activity that you did before anyone told you what to do? _____

o   What was the first thing you made, created, or played with?

_____

o   Who was the first grownup that you tried to imitate—what was he or she doing that got your attention?

_____

o   How did you express it in your child-like way?

_____

Select one of your gifts to pursue, but consider yourself blessed if you only have one gift.

Multi-talented individuals can experience both a blessing and a curse from having multiple areas of giftedness. They often have so many talents and gifts that it is often hard for them to choose among them.

Name the gift you will pursue. Write it here:

_____
_____
_____

My dad once told me:

"Successful people are those who find one thing to do and stick with it. They do it over and over again until they become good at it."

An internationally known, self-made multi-millionaire gave me some good advice. I boastfully told him that I had three revolutionary ideas to pursue. He told me. "Good. Now choose one of those ideas to make happen."

Nothing beats the power of focus.

Set Preliminary Goals.
Highly successful people set goals and write them down. There is great power in a written goal. When written down, goal statements are transformed from mere ideas into unstoppable plans of action.

Write 3 goals.
Verb
(Write one word which describes the action you will take)
Which one,
How many
or what quantity?
What
To what
degree,
standards, or conditions
By When

Execute your plan. Remember the advice the multi-millionaire gave me. Select ONE of those goals. Write down an action plan that will help you to meet the goal you selected.

➢ Write 3 goals

➢ Choose a verb
    o (Write one word that describes the action you will take)

➢ State: which one, how many, or what quantity?

➢ Tell: what, to what degree, using which standards, or with what conditions"

➢ Identify time frame: by when?

Review and re-evaluate your goals, when necessary.

- Periodically evaluate the steps you've taken.
- Determine what worked and what did not.
- Celebrate your successes, no matter how small.
- Recalibrate your plans and if necessary, adjust your goals.

Tap into external resources.
- Link yourself to greatness.
- Find a mentor in the area or field that you have selected. By hearing their stories, you can glean strength and guidance.

It doesn't matter really which field you choose. Choose something you enjoy. But do it to the best of your ability.

Finally . . . .

Look for waymarks on your path to success:

There are three levels of success. They are:

Level 1: Self-worth—you will feel this when you begin to fulfill your life's purpose.

Level 2: Social worth—you will obtain this when you contribute to society or when you become philanthropic. Give people something that they are not willing to pay for; teach your craft to others. That contributes to your social worth.

Level 3: Immortal worth—this happens when others imitate you, or copy you or preserve your accomplishments. Most people never have the opportunity to know their immortal worth. Therefore, give "flowers" to those who have inspired you while they can still bask in the fragrance.

When are we most successful? When we apply our shoulder to the wheel, press to the mark of the high calling of excellence, go the extra mile, or "stick to the wicket".

Someone rightfully quipped, "the only place success comes before work is in the dictionary."

Apply yourself, work hard. Follow your star. Anticipate success as you joyfully work to fulfill your destiny.

These are the hallmarks of hope.

ENDNOTES

[1]   Hope and Faith are similar terms, but a look at their Greek origins explains the difference:

HOPE—Elpis
from a primary elpo (to anticipate, usually with pleasure)
Noun-feminine

Tit 1:2   In hope of eternal life, which God, that cannot lie, promised before the world began;

Tit 2:13 Looking for that blessed hope, and the glorious appearing of the great God and our Saviour Jesus Christ;

Tit 3:7   That being justified by his grace, we should be made heirs according to the hope of eternal life.

Who against hope believed in hope, that he might become the father of many nations, according to that which was spoken, so shall thy seed be.

> For whatsoever things were written aforetime were written for our learning, that we through patience and comfort of the scriptures might have hope.

> Ro 15:13 Now the God of hope fill you with all joy and peace in believing, that ye may abound in hope, through the power of the Holy Ghost.

Sources:
http://www.biblestudytools.com/Lexicons/Greek/grk.cgi?number+1679&version=kjv and *http://www.biblestudytools.com/Lexicons/Greek/freqdisp.cgi?book=tit&number=1680&count=3&version=kjv*

FAITH—Pistis
conviction of the truth of anything, belief; in the NT of a conviction or belief respecting man's relationship to God and divine things, generally with the included idea of trust and holy fervour born of faith and joined with it

a. relating to God
   1. the conviction that God exists and is the creator and ruler of all things, the provider and bestower of eternal salvation through Christ

b. relating to Christ
   1. a strong and welcome conviction or belief that Jesus is the Messiah, through whom we obtain eternal salvation in the kingdom of God

c. the religious beliefs of Christians

d. belief with the predominate idea of trust (or confidence) whether in God or in Christ, springing from faith in the same

   2. fidelity, faithfulness

      a. the character of one who can be relied on

Sources:
http://www.searchgodsword.org/lex/grk/view.cgi?number=1680 and http://www.searchgodsword.org/lex/grk/view.cgi?number=4102

[2] http://www.bible-history.com/isbe/Q/QUEEN+MOTHER/. and http://jwa.org/encyclopedia/article/hamutal-bible
According to these sources, the position of Queen Mother, that is, mother of the King, was a very powerful position, moreso even than wife of the king because the society of the day was polygamous.

[3] Asa is considered to be a good King, notwithstanding the evil practice of his mother Maachah, for he tore these idols down.

[4] 2nd Commandment of the Ten Commandments found in Exodus 20: 5-6 speaks also to the wrath of God as a result of the iniquity of the fathers and sons to the third and fourth generations.

5   Sir Walter Scott (1771-1832), Scottish poet and author in Marmion,
     Canto vi. Stanza 17.

6   White, Ellen G. (1940). The Desire of Ages. Omaha: Pacific Press
     Publishing Association., p. 720.

REFERENCES

Cruden, Alexander, A.M. 1968. *Cruden's Complete Concordance to the Old and New Testaments.* Grand Rapids: Zondervan.

Chronology of the History of Israel: A chronological chart of the people, places and time of Israel, Source Unknown. A footnote on the chart states the following: The basis for this chart was created by Wil Pound and was downloaded from his internet site, www.abideinchrist.com."

Note: I used this chart to cross-reference dates in my own analysis and chart that appears in this chapter. My chart was produced before seeing Wil Pound's chart and is distinguished by listing the parents of each king, the lineage of the mother, and the age of the king when he began to reign. All information for the chart I produced was derived from a study of I & II Kings, I & II Chronicles, and Jeremiah.

Frank Klassen, 1975. *The Chronology of The Bible.* Nashville: Regal Publishers, Inc.

The Holy Bible Authorized King James Version (KJV), Crown Reference Edition, 1985. Nashville: Holman Bible Publishers.

Lockyear, Herbert. 1958. *All the Men of the Bible.* Grand Rapids: Zondervan

Vine, W.E., Unger, Merrill F. and William White, Jr. 1985. *Vine's Expository Dictionary of the Bible.* Nashville: Thomas Nelson, Inc.

Online Sources:
Davidiy, Yair. (accessed in 20008).
http://www.searchgodsword.org/lex/grk/view.
cgi?number=1680
http://www.searchgodsword.org/lex/grk/view.
cgi?number=4102
Role of the Queen mother:
http://jwa.org/encyclopedia/article/hamutal-bible

Love

Mothering is a work of love. Despite evidence unseen, mothers must maintain fervent hope while preparing their children for success. This unwavering display of support is a form of unconditional love, known in the Bible as agapé.

The Bible's Women of Love will show you how to:

- discuss the five principles of unconditional or agapé love.
- recall the stories of Biblical women who used these five principles as they raised the children they adopted.
- explore ways to demonstrate agapé principles as we "mother" our children, both natural and adopted.

The Five Agapé Principles:
* Compassion * Provision   * Inclusion
* Nurture   * Preparation

Women of Love
Show Unconditional Love

Mothering is a work of love. Despite evidence unseen, mothers must maintain fervent hope while preparing their children for success. This unwavering display of support is a form of unconditional love, known in the Bible as agapé love.

During the mothering process, the fruits of motherhood are often not discernible. Paul probably had mothers in mind when he penned the famous words of inspiration, "Now, faith is the substance of things hoped for, the evidence of things not seen" (Hebrews 11:1). When things go awry, a mother may freely claim the promise found in this scripture as she speaks her child's name aloud: "Child of mine, you are the substance of things hoped for, the evidence of things not seen. God is still working on you."

As we spend time reflecting on the topic of "Mothering" and emphasize the need for unconditional love in the process, we will:

- discuss the five principles of unconditional love (agapé).

- hear the stories of Biblical women who used these five principles as they raised their adopted children. (These adoptive mothers of the Bible were: Pharaoh's daughter, Queen Tahpenes, and Jehosheba).

and

- explore ways to demonstrate the principles of unconditional or agapé love as we mother our own children, both natural and adopted.

"You've got to love them like God sends them," I once heard a wise woman say about children.

My grandmother, Lucille, was a master at this concept. She had a roomy house, but an even bigger heart. Before apartment-dwelling for Negro college students was possible or affordable, Lucille often provided housing for those who wished to further their education in our hometown of Nashville, Tennessee. And when she spread the table, all were welcome. On Sunday after church, every holiday, and anytime people showed up, Lucille made everyone feel at home. The college professor and the hustler; the honest and the thief; the liar and the truth teller; from the richest to the poorest; the heterosexual and the homosexual; all were welcome.

When she died, I realized that there was no longer a neutral ground of acceptance and that, perhaps, the greatest lesson she taught us was not how to prepare a meal for a crowd, serve with the finest china or decorate one's home with the flavor of an antebellum mansion. Rather, Grandma Lucille's greatest lesson and her legacy were to show us how to accept others and how to show unconditional love.

Bible writer Ellen White infers that true love (unconditional love) is a high and holy principle. It is the bedrock of our greatest emotional need: acceptance. But the purpose of this unconditional love is broader than making a person feel validated and acceptable 'as they are.' As man is embraced unconditionally, he learns to extend such love to others, embracing them unconditionally. The ultimate aim of unconditional love is to lead the giver and, perhaps, the receivers of unconditional love toward God. The Bible calls this type of love "agape."

Agapé is the love God shows when He continually embraces sinful, imperfect man. It is the kind of love He commands us to have for each other: "A new commandment I give unto you . . . that ye agapaō[1] one another as I have agapaō you." (John 13:34). Jesus was testing Peter to see whether He could entrust the care of the new converts, His lambs, to Peter. This is the same question that God asks each of us when He places children in our care: "Do you love me? if so, nurture the little ones that I have given to you."

I recall a sermon I once heard by Pastor Barry Black. In essence, he said:

"Agapé love is not easy. It's not that kind of love that you slip, trip, and fall into. Agapé requires a high level of maturity. For most people, it is not easily turned on. It is the kind of love that remains after you could have been turned off. Agapé is not blind. It clearly sees the unworthiness of the recipient and matches it with benevolence. [Agapé is the kind of love that a mother must have toward her children.] Of course, it is easier to love a child when you know the source of its DNA, when it has your eyes and his smile. Most mothers can love the lovable—the obedient, respectful child. Most can even find some redeeming quality in the unlovable, when it is their own biological child.[4]" [paraphrased]

But love that is shown when a woman embraces a child birthed by another woman is the kind of love that is highly esteemed by God and man. That is also agapé.

That type of agapé is written about in scripture in Exodus 2, I Kings 11, and II Kings 12. These chapters give mothers the five principles of showing agapé, not only to their adoptive children, but to all. In child-rearing, agapé is shown through

- Compassion
- Provision
- Inclusion
- Nurture
- Preparation

These are the five principles of agapé love.

Five Agapé Principles

Compassion

Provision

Inclusion

Nurture

Preparation

First, let's talk about Compassion

If you have already taken a child into your home, you have exhibited compassion. Like Pharaoh's daughter, you have had your 'heart strings' touched by a child in need. Exodus 2 describes the adoption of the three-month old baby Moses by Pharaoh's daughter. She spotted a small ark, nestled among the tall reeds on the river's edge.

Exodus Chapter 2, verse 6 says: And when she had opened it, she saw the child: and, behold, the babe wept. And she had compassion on him, and said, This is one of the Hebrew's children.

Moses' sister, Miriam, who was watching the scene from afar spoke up and said, "Shall I get a Hebrew woman to nurse him for you?" Once he was weaned and had grown a bit, the boy child was brought back to the palace and became the son of Pharaoh's daughter. Because of compassion the baby in the bulrush ark, a boy born into Hebrew slavery, was spared an early death and nurtured by his own mother, Jochabed.[5] Moreover, he was groomed for success by a robust Egyptian education, the luxuries of freedom, and life in a palace.

Years later, another Pharaoh's household provided a home for an 'adopted' child. From a previous Bible study you may remember King David's military commander, Joab. He was the officer commanding the battle in which Uriah the Hittite (Bathsheba's husband) was killed[6]. When David's army waged war against the Edomites, his commander, Joab, was responsible for ensuring the death of the injured and killing all of the remaining adult Edomite males. The Bible records that Joab searched the land for six months to ensure that all were dead. However, Hadad, the son of the Edomite King, and several of the king's servants escaped Joab's watch. Hadad and a few others escaped to Midian, to Paran and then later to Egypt where he was rescued by the Pharaoh. The rescue of Hadad is another Biblical example that began with compassion.

Now on to our second Agapé Principle: Provision

Provision secures the basic needs for the child, which are food, clothing, shelter, education and the development of the child's talents and natural gifts. Of course, provision is situational and must be based on the economic means that the family has. Far more important than the economics, however, is the emotional support that the home provides. If one area of provision must be lacking, let it be the extras that money can buy rather than the love, display of genuine affection, and the balance between discipline and approval.

In our previously mentioned Bible story of the young Hadad, we find an example of provision. When they arrived in Egypt, the Pharaoh provided for Hadad and the small troop of refugees, giving them land, a house, and other provisions. While in Egypt, Hadad grew up. He found so much favor with Pharaoh that Pharaoh allowed Hadad to marry his sister-in-law, the sister of Queen Tahpenes. Inclusion is the third Agapé Principle.

Continuing with the story of Hadad, we move to the third principle, inclusion. Queen Tahpenes' sister bore a child for Hadad. The boy's name was Genubath. Queen Tahpenes weaned the child in Pharaoh's house and raised him in Pharaoh's household among the other sons of Pharaoh. (I Kings 11: 20-21). The term *"among the other sons of Pharaoh"* indicates that, with regard to Genubath, the queen practiced inclusion.

Inclusion is the area in which many of us fall short. Often the child is physically present in the household, but is emotionally excluded. What does it really mean to include a child? Inclusion means making the child a part of the activities of the family. It also includes ensuring that the child feels that he is a part of the family. By planning some activities that appeal to the child's interests, you can ensure that the child feels validated. Showing genuine interest in his programs and activities also signals inclusion. Inclusion also suggests that the doors within the home will be open more often than they are closed. When opinions are being shared, inclusion ensures that you won't leave out the child's ideas.

Nurture and Preparation are Agapé Principles Four and Five

One of the distinguishing characteristics of mammals from other classes within the animal kingdom is that they nurture their young. It is through the nurturing process that mammals such as human beings learn to provide nurture for the generations that follow. Among humans, nurturing goes beyond nutrition. When properly done, it shapes the emotional well-being and equips your child to be a functional member of society. In fact, it determines how the child will interact in his future relationships, family, and in the workplace. It will determine whether he can participate in give-and-take relationships, respect authority, and obey society's laws. It largely determines how well your child will do in school and, to some degree, how well she will be able to work in organizational settings. Proper nurturing sets boundaries, cultivates a respect for authority and develops the moral decision-making abilities.

As our final Biblical example, Jehosheba and her husband, the priest Jehoida, raised the infant Joash for six years. They nurtured and prepared him to become the rightful king of Judah in the lineage of King Ahaziah.

The baby Joash had survived a bloody massacre that, presumably, had killed all of the male heirs to King Ahaziah's throne. When Ahaziah's half-sister, Jehosheba, found the baby Joash in the rubble, she took him and his nurse to her home. There, Aunt Jehosheba[7] and her husband, Priest Jehoida, nurtured Joash and prepared him to take the throne. By age seven Joash had been trained in the practice of righteous principles, decision-making, self-management, and the lessons of obedience. The Bible records in II Kings 12:2, "And Jehoash did what was right in the sight of the Lord all his days wherein Jehoida the priest instructed him."

Adoptive parents who are attentive to the proper nurturing and preparation of a child can wield a powerful influence for the betterment of a child and the society of which the child is a part. As a result of the labor of Jehosheba and Jehoida, Joash was sufficiently nurtured and prepared for service. He was able to become king at the tender age of seven years old. Young Joash, therefore, replaced his evil grandmother, Athalia, who had become queen and ruler of Judah after her son, King Ahaziah, had died. In so doing, Joash began the process of restoring the lineage of David in the progression of the kings of Judah. This fulfilled the true genealogy of Jesus Christ[8] as our Saviour and King.

Summary

All five principles—compassion, provision, inclusion, nurture and preparation—are vitally important as you mother the children in your care.

There are many children today who are in need. Blessed among all mothers is one who can open her heart and home to a child someone else has birthed. Blessed, still, is the mother who will train that child in the righteous principles of the Almighty God and, thereby raise human beings who bring Him honor and enrich society.

Of course, it is not every woman's purpose to become an adoptive parent, but we can all make a determination to develop agapé toward the children whose lives we touch. Whether it is your own child, a neighborhood child or children that you teach at school, agapé is the love that will win hearts to Jesus Christ—through service, not sermons.

Does the application of these principles ensure that the child will never make a mistake or follow the wrong path? No. In fact, the Bible records acts of aggression committed by both Moses and Joash in their later years:[8]

As Moses grew up, he became increasingly troubled by the conditions of slavery in Egypt. One day he became angry when he saw an Egyptian beating one of his Hebrew countrymen who was a slave. Moses killed the Egyptian and buried him in the sand. When he learned that Pharaoh was displeased and sought to kill him also, Moses fled to Midian. (Read Exodus 2:11-22).

After his uncle, priest Jehoida, died, Joash began to lead Judah into idolatrous practices. Jehoida's son, the prophet Zechariah, spoke out against what Joash was doing. As a result, Joash issued the order to have Zechariah killed by stoning. As a result of their idolatry and the stoning of God's prophet, God allowed Judah to be invaded by the Syrians. The Syrian captivity was so harsh that the people of Judah rebelled and blamed Joash. They executed judgment against him and his servants killed Joash in his own bed. By his actions, Joash forfeited a burial in the sepulchres among the other kings of Judah. (See II Chronicles 24:25).

Some may then ask, "What is the point of mothering with the agapé principles if there are no guarantees? Why go to the trouble of nurturing, preparing, and providing for a child who will not live up to the set standard—or who may veer off the path?"

The scriptures attest that "all have sinned and come short of the glory of God . . . but the gift of God is eternal life."[9] Therein lies our answer. Each of us is born once without our choice. But our failings give us the opportunity to choose to be reborn in God's image. The early training received by way of the agapé principles serve as an 'emotional launch pad' for esteeming that which is good and of God.

Some adoptive mothers, including one who confided in me, have mixed feelings when the children they have adopted want to seek out their biological families. This is to be expected. The Bible records that when Hadad found out that both King David and his Commander, Joab were dead, Hadad wanted to return home. In I Kings 11:22, the Pharaoh expressed the sentiment of many adoptive parents:

> "What have you lacked here with me that you must seek in your own country?"

Hadad's answer to the Pharaoh seeks to reassure adoptive parents:

> "Nothing: howbeit, let me go in any wise."

In this respect, parents and others reading this book may ponder, "What good is it for me to show compassion and inclusion if it won't bring loyalty?" They may also wonder, "Why does my child want to seek out those who lacked compassion and did not, for whatever reason, include him?"

My answer is this: your works bear witness to your faithfulness to the calling and the purpose that has become yours to fulfill. If we follow the agapé principles and show compassion, make provision, and demonstrate inclusion, nurturing and preparation, we will be able to proudly answer when the Lord says to each of us, "Woman, where is the flock that was given thee, thy beautiful flock?" Jeremiah 13: 20.

For me, this agapé ministry is applied to the two daughters that God gave me and those He blesses to come to our home. I have imperfections and flaws. I am a long way away from loving like Christ but I strive toward agapé because I have been loved with agapé.

Each of us can lead a child to Christ, by showing a love that won't quit, won't fade, and won't give up until in their countenances we see Christ glorified.

Think About It 🗩

Did Peter ever reach the ability to agapaō?

Is it possible to agapaō without being taken advantage of?

Is it practical in today's world to practice a servant-based love ?

What are the barriers that prevent most from bringing an adopted child into their households?

Should one spouse pursue adoption of a child despite the reluctance of the other?

Can adoption work with the biological parents and the adoptive parents both playing active roles in a child's life? Consider the arrangement between Pharaoh's daughter and Jochabed, Moses' mother. Support or refute this idea.

Practicing the Agapé Principles
Worksheet

Compassion asks me to identify and examine the pain, as well as the cause of the pain, that a child is feeling and try to help alleviate it. Pharaoh's daughter was able to look at a weeping baby and determine that he needed to be nursed and nurtured. Sometimes a child's needs are not so easily discerned. In those cases, try to get to the root cause of the pain by asking the child to express his feelings verbally or in writing, perhaps in a diary. If the child is very young, you may encourage him to create a picture journal and ask him to draw faces expressing the feelings he is having. Or if the child is artistic, encourage her to draw pictures showing how she is feeling or what has caused the feelings she is having. If the child is not artistic at all, you can draw faces (called emoticons) that show a variety of expressions. Then your child can simply circle the face that best expresses his or her own emotion. Empathize with the child's feelings by giving appropriate feedback to the child. This dialogue will help to build trust, thereby making it easier for the child to open up and attempt to express his/her pain on future occasions.

In the following spaces, write your plan to help the hurting child in your care:

1.

2.

3.

Provision secures the basic needs for children—physical, emotional and maturational. Some needs will remain the same. Others will change as the child gets older. What are your thoughts about provision? What needs should be considered? Food, clothing, shelter, a stable home environment and a sense of belonging are the immediate physical and emotional needs. A child's maturational needs are related to desirable social qualities and acceptable behavioral characteristics. In what ways can you provide an environment for your child to develop such maturation?

In the following spaces, write down the things you will provide for your child.

1.

2.

3.

Inclusion says to the child, "You are important to me. I am interested in what you are interested in." As a child grows up, the definition of inclusion becomes, "You are a part of us. We are not complete without you." At the early stages, inclusion is felt when the parent pauses from a busy routine to play on the floor with a child, getting into the mindset and choice of activities the child selects. In play, children reveal a lot about their interests, temperament and what delights them. When you are involved in the child's world, the child is likely to trust you and later agree to be involved in your selection of activities. Inclusion is felt when the child accompanies the family on outings, car trips and other vacations. This sets up a healthy give-and-take exchange that broadens as the child matures.

What aspects of your life are you willing to share with your child? What can you do to build trust with your child? What inclusion activities will you plan for the child in your care? Write them in the spaces below:

I make sure this child feels part of our family unit by:

1.

2.

3.

Nurture of their young is one of the identifying characteristics of mammals. As humans, we both nurse and nurture our young. Nurture, in its very basic sense, is the provision of milk and suckling. But it must include cuddling, talking, affirming and reassuring so that the child simultaneously experiences healthy physical and emotional growth. Nurturing the toddler and older child demands different levels of nurturing. Like dominoes, other needs present themselves and, as a part of nurturing, must be met: different levels of compassion; inclusion; and the child's sense of security that your provision brings. As humans, we tend to nurture in the ways that we were nurtured and we repeat those lessons, whether good or bad. By planning how nurturing will take place with your children, you and your partner can overcome many non-productive actions and replace them with psychologically healthy alternatives.

What did nurture look like in your family of origin? What did it look like in your spouse's family of origin? What are the challenges you have in nurturing your own children? If you have a foster child or have adopted an older child, what appears to have been missing in the child's family of origin?

In the spaces below, record the special form of nurturing that your child best responds to.

1.

2.

3.

Preparation will ensure that one day your child will be able to make it without you. The aspects of development we focus on is based upon our belief system and our own ability.

On one hand, preparation is as simple as ensuring the child possesses independent living skills such as being able to launder one's own clothing and being able to prepare a simple meal. It also includes the acquisition of formal education; a skill, a trade, or other career training; and practical social skills like decision-making. If you are religious, it also means giving opportunities for the child to 'apply' the scriptural truths that they can recite so well.

List the things that you will do to prepare this child to make it on his or her own in the future.

Think about how you can prepare your child for his/her:

Life Purpose

1.

2.

'Kingdom' Purpose

3.

4.

Something Extra . . . .

A woman who uses the 5 Agapé Principles in the workplace will be more effective when she employs these principles.

The following pages will tell you to apply them in the workplace. You will be able to build relationships with those whom you have been charged to lead. You will inspire a "shine" that I like to call "Gemspark."

 # You can inspire Gemspark in your employees

Your co-workers . . . . your students . . . . your family members . . . . yourself

Using the 5 Principles of Agapé Leadership

Gemspark—the potential to make a contribution; everyone has it. As manager, a teacher or a family leader, you must tap into it. Do this by using the Agapé Principles.

Agapé Principles

Women have many roles in society:

In the home as mothers, grandmothers, aunties, and caregivers. In the workplace as leaders, teachers, and managers of employees.

To bring out the best in all situations, they must minister to the heart of people. As such, they must show Agape love. They can do that by delivering these 5 principles:

Five Agapé Principles

Compassion

Provision

Inclusion

Nurture

Preparation

- Compassion
- Provision
- Inclusion
- Nurture
- Preparation

Compassion asks you to recognize what it took for your students, your employees or your coworkers to get to this point.

Point your student to services that can help them through difficult topics, subjects or issues. Help **students** to see their failures on a continuum. By showing a failure as a small part of one's academic life and an even smaller part of their overall life, you can add balance and inspire them to continue.

Employees want to do a good job. Sometimes life's mishaps prevent optimum performance. Develop good coaching skills that focus on job-specific behaviors. When the problems are not job-related, your local Employee Assistance Program can help.

Learn to measure greatness by point-to-point success.

Provision secures the basic needs for your learners or your office mates. What do they need to be productive?

For students, a well-designed syllabus, organized course content, consistent office hours, and a predictable demeanor can create the type of learning environment that promotes student success. Under these conditions, students can more easily chart their success in your course.

Your employees need proper tools to get the job done. In addition to physical tools, that also includes workspace and equipment. More importantly your employees need authority over the areas for which they are responsible. *Responsibility plus authority equals success.*

Inclusion says "you are valued here."

Create a vibrant educational environment that validates a student's prior learning and rewards **students** as they stretch toward new assignments and goals. Studies show that students are more likely to stay in school and graduate when: a student's sending school environment is validated and accepted by the receiving school and similarities between the two environments exist

Allow your **employees** to contribute to organizational goals in ways that show their strongest skills. Where possible, evaluate the ends, rather than the means. Keep your employees informed of changes and plans that affect the department. Provide access to meetings and departmental information to all levels of staff, unless the information is confidential.

Involvement creates a feeling of ownership.

Nurturing inspires the confidence that human beings need to take on the challenges that they will face. Always present a failure on a timeline, showing it as a small part of an entire life history. Give steps that will lead to success.

Teach your **students** new subjects by starting from the known and moving to the unknown. Coach them by suggesting possibilities that will help them to achieve success. The way you present their successes and failures will often determine their self-worth. Learn how to deliver bad news without making the student feel incapable of success in the future.

Nurturing helps **employees** to develop the confidence they need to tackle larger tasks. Nurturing your employees includes praise for a job well done, coaching and counseling an employee through difficult assignments, providing guidance and sometimes, just lending an ear.

Praise in public; reprimand in private.

Preparation provides for future success. By equipping others you can help them to achieve success today and provide the springboard for success for tomorrow.

Students who are well-prepared in your class will be able to learn more about your subject and any other subject in the future. Why? because you have given them the tools to learn.

As a manager, create a succession plan and then provide on-the-job-training that will allow your current **employees** to gain the required knowledge required to meet new job targets. Don't forget to give them a "no-risk" opportunity to try out these new skills. When you move up the organizational ladder yourself, you will have capable employees ready to assume your current position.

Knowledge plus Experience creates promotability.

Extend . . .

You can hear and read about the stories of Biblical women who used these five principles as they raised their adopted children. (These adoptive mothers of the Bible were: Pharaoh's daughter, Queen Tahpenes, and Jehosheba). *Mothers of Love* is available in paperback, e-book, and audio book formats. Of course, it is not every woman's purpose to become an adoptive parent, but we can all make a determination to develop "agape" toward those whose lives we touch. Whether it is your own child, a neighborhood child, children that you teach at school, or those whom you lead in the workplace, agapé is the love that will win hearts to Jesus Christ—through service, not sermons.

Summary

What does all of this mean? The five attributes of womanhood mean nothing if they do not help you to lead a more purpose-driven, spirit-filled life. It should help you to be more focused as you await the second coming of Jesus Christ—your vertical relationships, but each attribute should contribute something towards the quality of relationships you have horizontally, with other human beings.

Look for Hope , anticipate the best for others, doing what
you can to encourage and uplift. Protect yourself in your
relationships: be wise as a serpent, but harmless as a dove[9].
Love others with the heart of God, being a servant of God
brings the true joy out of life.

ENDNOTES

[1] Agapaō is the verb tense of agapé.

[2] This discussion of agapé is based on the definitions contained in Vine's Expository Dictionary of Biblical Words, pages 381-382.

[3] White, Ellen G., *The Adventist Home*, p. 50.
The full citation read, "True love is a high and holy principle altogether different in character from that love which is awakened by impulse, and,which suddenly dies when severely tested.
Love is a plant of heavenly growth, and it must be fostered and nourished. Affectionate hearts, truthful, loving words, will make happy families and exert an elevating influence upon all who come within the sphere of their influence.

[4] Black, Barry. (1988?), "The Bubble of Self-Confidence," an audiotape.

[5] Read Exodus 2: 5-10 to find out how Miriam, the older sister of Moses was instrumental in arranging for their own mother Jochabed to nurse Moses. Read more about Miriam in *Nothing New Under the Sun*: *Lessons on Living from Women of the Bible*, Chapter 4—Sibling Rivalry, also by author of this book.

[6] Read more about King David, Bathsheba, Uriah, and Joab in *Nothing New Under the Sun: Lessons on Living from Women of the Bible*, Chapter 3-Sexual Violation, also by author of this book.

[7] The Bible lists Jehosheba as a daughter of King Jehoram. King Ahaziah was the son of King Jehoram. King Ahaziah and Jehosheba were siblings. Therefore, Jehosheba was Joash's aunt. Read more on this subject in 2Chronicles 22 and Mothers of Hope, also by the author of this book.

[8] Athalia was the daughter of King Ahab and *Jezebel*. Athalia married Jehoram, who was the son of good King Jehoshaphat. Athalia gave birth to Ahaziah, who followed his father Jehoram, as King of

Judah. Jehoshaphat, Jehoram and Ahaziah were of the lineage of David. However, Athalia, being the daughter of pagan King Ahab and Baal worshipper Jezebel, was not of the lineage of David. Therefore, Athalia was not a rightful heir to the throne of Judah, even though she seized the throne at her son's death. Joash was of the lineage of David, as he was Ahaziah's son. When he replaced his grandmother, Athalia on the throne, the rulership was rightfully restored to the lineage of David. However, in the Bible (Matthew Chapter 1:7-14), neither of the kings whose heritage can be traced to Athalia or her parents, King Ahab and Jezebel are recorded in the genealogy of Christ. Those rulers of Judah whose names are omitted from the genealogy of Christ are: King Ahaziah, Queen Mother Athalia, King Joash and King Amaziah. Read more on this subject in the Bible, found in II Chronicles Chapter 22 and *Mothers of Hope*, also by the author of this book. See the family tree on the next page.

9   Read Moses' story in Exodus Chapter 2 beginning at verse 11. Read about the demise of Joash in II Chronicles, Chapter 24, beginning at verse 17.

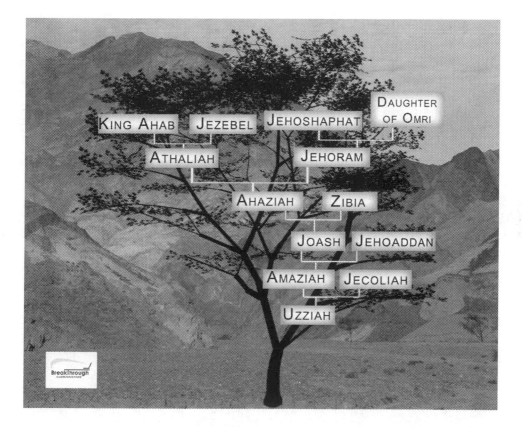

REFERENCES

The Holy Bible Authorized King James Version (KJV), Crown Reference Edition, 1985. Nashville: Holman Bible Publishers.

Lockyear, Herbert. 1958. *All the Men of the Bible*. Grand Rapids: Zondervan.

Vine, W.E., Unger, Merrill F. and William White, Jr. 1985. *Vine's Expository Dictionary of the Bible*. Nashville: Thomas Nelson, Inc.

NOTE: The discussion of John 13 was inspired by a sermon given by Pastor Barry Black, Chaplain of the United States Marine Corps. The author further researched this passage of scripture using *Vine's Expository Dictionary of Biblical Terms* and applied its concepts to the Biblical Women discussed herein.

BIBLE PROMISE FOR YOU

Lovest (agapaō) thou me? . . . . feed my sheep.

John 21:15

Wisdom

Knowledge comes from many sources, but wisdom comes exclusively from God.

In this chapter, we will discover that Women of Wisdom:

- Go on God's errands
- Pass the test of a *true prophetess*
- Participate in mentoring relationships (Naomi and Ruth)
- Make Decisions guided by Wisdom
- Provide Godly Leadership (Deborah)
- Discern True Prophets and Prophetesses
- Handle their Business Affairs Wisely (Lydia)
- Use Their Family Resources to Further the Gospel (Priscilla)
- Provide Leadership when they are Heads of Household (Daughters of Zelophehad)

Wisdom is the principal thing; therefore get wisdom: and with all thy getting get understanding. Proverbs 4:4-6

Women of Wisdom
Follow God's Lead

Where does wisdom come from?

A little girl sat at her grandmother's dressing table. She dusted her face with loose powder, sprayed a matronly scent, and then ran her grandmother's comb through her own hair. She glanced in the mirror and swung both feet around the bench at the same moment, exclaiming, "Granny . . . . look . . . . I have a gray hair."

"That's your wisdom, my dear."

"Granny," the little girl thought aloud, "then you have too much wisdom!"

The grandmother gave a hearty bout of laughter and replied, "You can never have too much wisdom, my child. In life, you will need it all—and then some."

As amusing as that story might be, the Bible lets us know that wisdom doesn't come from gray hairs. It comes from God. Here's what the Bible says about wisdom:

> "And God gave Solomon wisdom and understanding exceeding much, and largeness of heart, even as the sand that is on the sea shore."
>
> I Kings 4:29

> "Only the Lord give thee wisdom and understanding, and give thee charge concerning Israel, that thou mayest keep the law of the Lord thy God."
>
> I Chronicles 22:12

You may have noticed that when referring to wisdom, the Bible passages above also mention the word, understanding.

However, of the two words—wisdom and understanding—wisdom is the most primary, predominant, and pre-eminent. In fact, the Bible says, this:

> Wisdom is the principal thing; therefore get wisdom: and
> with all thy getting get understanding. (Proverbs 4:7)

What is the difference between wisdom and understanding? By searching a Hebrew Lexicon like Strong's Concordance, we can derive a deep understanding of the meaning of the words, wisdom and understanding in Proverbs 4:7.

Wisdom
In the text, Proverbs 4:7, the Hebrew word for wisdom is Chokmah (COKE-mah). Strong's Concordance says that Chokmah is seen as keen ability in administration, skillfulness in war, shrewdness, prudence in religious matters, and the demonstration of ethical behaviour. Each of these characteristics requires good judgment. Chokmah is the kind of wisdom that can be seen by others. When a woman possesses Chokmah, it causes her to exercise good judgment. She will be seen to be doing a good job.

When a woman has Chokmah, it causes others to say, "Wow! Look at that woman. She is on top of her game! She is wise beyond her years, or She's nobody's fool."

Wisdom is therefore judged by what is demonstrated. Because humans look upon the outward appearance of things (1Samuel 16:7), our display of wisdom—or lack of it—will be the yardstick by which our lives will be evaluated: "What did we do?" and "How well did we do it?"

Understanding
As with wisdom, there are also many Hebrew words that are translated in English as "understanding." In scriptures such as Proverbs 4:7, the word "understanding" is the Hebrew word, Biynah (BEE-nah).

Biynah is an uncommon level of understanding. Biynah is more than comprehension. It goes beyond ordinary understanding. This level of understanding is probably more accurately translated as discernment. It is the ability to grasp the most obscure parts of an issue. It is Biynah which gives Chokmah its "wow" factor. When a woman understands on the "Biynah" level, her judgment and manner of living is characterized by "Chokmah."

Solomon demonstrates his understanding

To illustrate the dynamic relationship between Biynah and Chokmah, I would like to recall the story of King Solomon and two women who were arguing over the ownership of a baby. In this Bible story, King Solomon, the wisest man who ever lived, demonstrated his deep understanding of the maternal instinct and, thereby, gave one of the wisest solutions to conflict that has ever been recorded. Here is the story:

In the days of King Solomon, two women lived in the same house. Each woman had given birth to a baby. One baby died. Both women then began to claim the live baby as their own. They came to King Solomon. Solomon acted with wisdom, but he based his actions on a keen understanding of the most obscure parts of the issue.

Mere, ordinary understanding may have caused the king to ask for evidence, establish the facts regarding the time and place of the baby's disappearance, and other factors of proof. But King Solomon's discernment went beyond that. Because he truly understood the nature of motherhood and the maternal instinct, he ordered the live baby to be cut in half. His solution would grant each woman one-half of the live baby. One woman reacted appropriately and could not bear the thought of slicing the baby in half. King Solomon deemed her to be the true mother and delivered the baby to her arms. His wisdom was evident (chokmah). King Solomon used good judgment and solved the problem skillfully. His deep understanding (biynah) and discernment, however, were the keys which enabled him to choose the most effective course of action. Chokmah and Biynah. Wisdom and understanding. When we have both, we will be noticed by our fellow man for having uncommon perception, intuition, and judgment. We will have command of our resources and do things in a marvelously excellent way.

Summary

Chokmah (Wisdom) is the outward display of good judgment. It is what others see us do. Biynah (Understanding) is the control center that directs our actions.

Chokmah + Biynah = An execution of judgment that is based on an uncommonly good reasoning of the facts.

How can a woman obtain this type of Wisdom?
The good news is that we can all gain this type of wisdom. When God gives you a task, He will also give you the wisdom and understanding to do it well. The Bible assures us of this in the following text:

> "Then wrought Bezaleel and Aholiab, and every wise hearted man, in whom the Lord put wisdom and understanding to know how to work all manner of work for the service of the sanctuary, according to all that the Lord had commanded. Exodus 36:1

Whether it is a new job, the position of wife, or the charge of motherhood, God will place within you both the wisdom and understanding needed to accomplish each task.

If you have been given a task or if any task falls upon you to do, don't be dismayed. If you do not know how to do it, ask God. He will generously and liberally grant you the wisdom and understanding that are necessary to complete the task.

"If any of you lack wisdom, let him ask of God, that
giveth to all men liberally, and upbraideth not; and it
shall be given him. James 1:5

A Woman's Decisions must be guided by Wisdom

This book is written for all women, but it has special significance
to those who are standing at a crossroad in life, those who are
approaching age 50, planning to be age 50 one day, or stand, as it
were, on a number line and glance at 50 over their left shoulder.

To those ladies, I affirm, "Wisdom is a muscle that, when exercised
over time, will help you to land in high places. Without it, you
may repeat the same life lessons over and over, without growth.
And sometimes you will never have a second chance."

With respect to time, there is one message that I offer to my
fellow 50-somethings and those who are approaching it:

"This stage of your life is not a dress rehearsal." There is very
little time left for making poor decisions. There is no more time
for recovery from bad choices. Each choice must be principled
and God-led. Each move you make must be a wise one.

If you lack wisdom, ask God for it. If you have little wisdom, ask
God. He will grant you more.

There is also no time to keep putting off doing the things that will
enhance your life and make your journey sweeter. No doubt, you
have worked hard. You have sacrificed for a family—perhaps,
you found it necessary to live up to your parents' expectations.
Maybe your sacrifices were for your husband, your children,
or both. In either case, you have done what was necessary to
enable your family to get to whatever point they are now. If your
children are educated—you helped to put them through school.
If your family owns a business or property—you worked in the
trenches, building, encouraging, managing, figuring, re-figuring
and doing whatever it took to make the best of your resources.

You've spent thousands of dollars on medical bills, braces, music lessons, camps, and school supplies—not to mention toys, and the other nice-to-haves.

Now that you are at the midpoint of your life, realize, "This time is for you, but you must exercise wisdom. Cover your gray hair if you like, but in the process, don't conceal your wisdom. The quality of the rest of your life depends on it."

This is also not the time for unbridled passions to take over one's life or to serve self with a cavalier disregard for God's principles:

> "For the wisdom of this world is foolishness with God."
> (I Corinthians 3:19)

The Bible also cautions against unwise behaviour:

> "There is a way which seemeth right to a man, but the end thereof are the ways of death." Proverbs 14:11-13 and Proverbs 16:25

Interestingly enough, that Bible verse is written twice in the book of Proverbs. This seems to say to the Bible reader, "if you missed it the first time, here it is, again."

It is God's reminder to us that when a woman will surrender her wishes to the will of God, she will emerge highly victorious and better off than if she had wielded her own way. Move, but only in the will of God.

How can a woman be certain of God's will?

I recommend this acid test:

> "To the law and to the testimony, if they speak not according to this word, it is because there is no light in them." Isaiah 8:20.

The law of which Isaiah speaks are the Ten Commandments. The testimony refers to the written testimonies of the major and minor prophets, from Moses to John, the Revelator, and all in between. In other words, if what you are considering or what you have devised in your heart breaks one of the Ten Commandments, don't bother with it. If the desire does not follow the counsel of the holy men of old who spake as God influenced them (II Peter 1:21), then the origin of the desire is spiritual wickedness. Remember, Satan is the prince of wickedness. Simply put, if God cannot support it fully, then it is of Satan.

Does it follow the		Yes?	No?
LAW	**Ten Commandments** *And God spake all these words saying, I am the Lord thy God, Thou shalt not have any gods before me . . .* **Exodus 20: 1-17** *Thy word have I hid in mine heart, that I might not sin against thee.* **Psalm 119:10-12** *Thy word is a lamp unto my feet, and a light unto my path.* **Psalm 119:105** *Sanctify then through thy truth: thy word is truth.* **John 17:16-18**		
TESTIMONY	**Contained in the books written by the prophets** *For the prophecy came not in old time by the will of man: but holy men of GOd spake as they were moved by the Holy Ghost.* **2 Peter 1:21** *The book of the law shall not depart out of my mouth but thou shalt meditate therein day and night, that thou mayest observe to do according to all that is written therein: for then thou shalt make thy way prosperous, and then thou shalt have good success.* **Joshua 1:7-9**		

BIBLE PROMISE FOR YOU

If any of you lack wisdom, let him ask of God, that giveth to all men liberally, and upbraideth not; and it shall be given him. James 1:5

Women of Wisdom in Modern Times

Throughout time, many women of wisdom have guided the course of human events. We can readily recite the names of those women who have captured the limelight: Senator Hillary Rhodham-Clinton[1], Prime Minister Margaret Thatcher, and the late Coretta Scott King. Their lives have been open books. Their wisdom and good judgment have been on display for all to see.

But, there are several unsung women of wisdom. Consider Sojourner Truth, an advisor in the abolitionist movement; Eleanor Roosevelt, wife and co-laborer with President Franklin D. Roosevelt; and even Amy, juvenile daughter of former President Jimmy Carter. These women did not hold a political office, but by their demonstrated abilities, management of public affairs, and perceived wisdom, they were consulted by men of position. Their contributions were hidden from our consciousness because they worked in the background or on the sideline. Yet, their opinions and counsel framed the actions that were taken by the men who consulted them.

Many of the women cited above, others that you may know and love, and the Biblical ones whose stories will follow may not have been actual mothers. I have associated them with and called them *Mothers* of Wisdom, because it is at their knee that we are nurtured and prepared to learn the lessons of wisdom. As Deborah proclaimed in Judges 5:7:

The inhabitants of the villages ceased, they ceased in Israel, until that I Deborah arose, that I arose a mother in Israel."

Women of Wisdom in Biblical Days

Several women in the Bible demonstrated wisdom and prophetic influence. Anna and Philip's Daughters in the New Testament were called prophetesses and Huldah, Miriam, and Deborah in the Old Testament were also prophetesses. They were called prophetesses because:

1. They acted and spoke on God's behalf.
2. Their lives were in harmony with God's law.
3. Their words confirmed the words that God had spoken to others, personally.
4. The things they said came to pass.

First, let us focus on the wisdom of the prophetess Deborah. Deborah's story is found in Judges chapters 4 and 5. Her skill in war tactics and her sage advice are the evidence of her wisdom. Her actions and words matched the words that God had spoken to Barak, an Israelite military general from the tribe of Naphtali. Therefore, she was not only wise, she was also a prophetess.

Women of Wisdom Provide Godly Leadership

Deborah served many roles. Not only was she a leader, a judge, and a respected woman, she was also a "Secretary of Defense" in Barak's military struggle against the Canaanites.

Deborah's most fascinating contribution is the wise strategy that she provided to Barak. Because she was connected to God, she was able to give Barak sound judgment which led to the military conquest of King Jabin's Canaanite army.

Furthermore, Deborah proved herself to be a prophetess because the advice that she gave to Barak was the same counsel that he had also received from God. Because Barak sought Deborah's assistance as he was considering going into battle, we could say that Deborah was a national security advisor, the "Condoleeza Rice" of Bible times. Prior to her appointment, former National Security Advisor Rice had spent time studying the tactics of America's adversaries[3] and was consulted by Commander-in-Chief George W. Bush. In a similar way, Deborah knew Canaanite strategy and was consulted by the Israelite Army commander, Barak.

Deborah was the wife of a man known as Lapidoth. But she is one of the women of Biblical times who was also known and respected on her own merits. Because of her wisdom, she was also a judge in Israel. Judges Chapter 4 records:

> 5 ... And the children of Israel came up to her [Deborah]
> for judgment under the palm trees.[4]" Judges 4:54

Over time, Deborah had apparently been hearing the pleas of the Israelites about Sisera, the fierce captain of king Jabin's army. The Lord had delivered the children of Israel into the hands of this Canaanite King. For 20 years God had allowed His people to be oppressed by Sisera (see Judges 4: 2). Because Deborah knew the word of the Lord concerning this situation, she called Barak to her and said to him:

> 6 ... hath not the Lord God of Israel commanded thee,
> saying, Go, and draw toward Mount Tabor, and take
> with thee 10,000 men of the children of Naphtali, and
> of the children of Zebulun?

Didn't He promise you that he would,

> 7 . . . . draw unto thee, to the river Kishon, Sisera
> the captain of Jabin's army, with his chariot and his
> multitude; and ... deliver him into thine hand?

Barak knew Deborah was right. Her counsel to him was in harmony with what he knew to be the word of God. God had previously given him the same message and Barak had refused to act upon it. But after confirmation from Deborah, Barak was ready for war. Judges 4: 8 records Barak's answer to Deborah:

> 8 ... Barak said unto Deborah, if thou will go with me
> then I will go: but if thou wilt not go with me, then I
> will not go.

Deborah agreed to go with Barak, but she told him that if she went, the victory of the battle would be in a woman's honor and not in his honor: God would let Sisera fall into the hands of a woman. Barak lacked the courage to go into battle without Deborah. Barak was obviously focused on the strength of Sisera's troops and was paralyzed by the mere thought of Sisera's fierce reputation, but Deborah confidently relied upon the word of God.

Deborah was effective in helping Barak to defeat Sisera's army because she knew the word of God. Her reliance upon it gave her courage. By definition, courage is "the quality of mind or spirit that enables a person to face difficulty.[5]" Deborah faced difficult situations, (and so can we) when we determine within ourselves to walk with God, to rely solely upon his word, trust not in our own resources, and allow Him to equip us with wisdom.

God has given us several texts to help us to discern whether we are following a true prophetess like Deborah, or whether we are dealing with a false prophet or prophetess.

The texts that support these statements are recorded in the *"Something Extra"* section. However, in summary, those who prophesy must:

o   uphold the Law
o   keep pagan practices separate from the doctrines of Christianity
o   be repentant of their own sins and accept appropriate discipline
o   be of good moral reputation
o   recognize Jesus Christ as Savior and soon-coming King
o   crucify self, ensuring that their prophecies yield to the word of God and the teachings of Christ
o   foretell things that actually come to pass
o   proclaim a message which aligns with what God has told you to do, previously

On the day of the battle, Barak must have been procrastinating, doubting himself and his troops. Or perhaps, he was lying aimlessly about while Sisera gathered together all of his chariots. Verse 13 tells us that Sisera gathered,

> 13 " . . . even 900 chariots of iron and all the people
> that were with him, from Arosheth of the Gentiles unto
> the river of Kishon.

Deborah provided leadership that was consistent with the word of God. Looking at Barak and seeing that he needed motivation, Deborah commanded Barak in one word only. She said, "Up." Incidentally, this was the same command that the three angels made to Lot when they were prodding him to leave Sodom in the book of Genesis. By these two examples, it seems that the word, 'Up' was used in those days to mean 'urgency'; in other words, 'move from this place; beware; peril and ruin are on the way.'

While reading the story of Deborah and Barak, it came to mind that Deborah was perhaps 'unimpressed' with Barak's slow inaction, his disobedience, and his lack of courage. She knew if Barak would just do what he had been told by God to do, her workload could be reduced significantly. Perhaps then, the Israelites would no longer come to her with complaints about Sisera's oppression of them.

As the Bible story continues, Deborah interrupted her daily routine and accompanied Barak to Tabor. Once she had his attention, she added to her imperative, "Up". She gave Barak a battle promise and a motivational nugget that were similar to the ones that God had given to Barak's forefathers in other battles:

> "for this is the day in which the Lord has delivered Sisera
> into thine hand: is not the Lord gone out before thee?"

At Deborah's urging, Barak went down from the Mount with his 10,000 troops after him. The battle was given to Barak according to verse 15, because the Lord discomfited[6] Sisera, and his entire chariot and all his hosts. Sisera was so afraid that he jumped off his chariot and fled away on foot. By this time, Barak had gained momentum and confidence. He continued to pursue Sisera's chariots and his hosts. Pursued by Barak's army, all the men in Sisera's troop fell upon their swords and died.

This battle was made easy because God frustrated the enemy. As a believer, I particularly take heart in God's ability to literally frustrate (discomfit) those who would harm me. I take courage in the fact that when I walk with the Lord, in the light of his word, that he will be my buckler[7] and shield. Join me in covenant with God. As we are obedient to Him, we can claim this promise from Deuteronomy 7:

> 18 "Thou shalt not be afraid of them: but shall well remember what the Lord thy God did unto Pharaoh and all of Egypt . . ." 21 Thou shalt not be affrighted at them: for the Lord thy God is among you, a mighty God and terrible.
>
> (Deuteronomy 7:18, 21)

The final verses of Judges 4 fulfill Deborah's prophecy that God would deliver Sisera into the hands of a woman. Sisera ran into the tent of Heber and Jael Hobar for shelter. (Jethro, Moses' father-in-law, was the son of Heber and Jael.) Once he became comfortable with Jael, Sisera asked her for a drink of water. Jael served him a drink of milk instead. While Sisera laid there resting from his exhausting escape on foot, Jael hammered a nail into his temple and killed him.

Perhaps, if God had simply told Barak that all he had to do to mortally destroy Sisera was to chase him into the tent of Heber and Jael, Barak may have had more courage to take on the battle a lot sooner.

> Barak's battle, like many of our own, is a test of our faith, not a demonstration of our ability.

Deborah was a motivator. That's what God is calling women of wisdom to do; to exert their influence to accomplish His will on earth, to inspire men and women to live up to their calling.

Women of Wisdom Handle their Business Affairs Wisely

<u>Lydia</u>
Lydia serves as a good example of a woman who exhibited business acumen *and* spiritual discernment. She was a woman of great wisdom and a seller of purple. There are mixed reviews on whether her product was a purple dye only or whether Lydia also sold fabric whose color was tinted by the dye. Lydia's first demonstration of wisdom was evident in that she used what was available to make a profitable living for her household.

Reportedly, the dye that Lydia marketed was extracted from the veins of a mollusk. In the body of the sea creature, the liquid was white. It was only when the liquid came in contact with the sun that it took on its purple hue.[8] Lydia used this liquid to make purple, a color that was quite useful in making priestly garments. Lydia was a classic entrepreneur in that she was able to take something from her existing supply and turn it into a separate, uncommon use. Or, she had been able to learn the trade of her kinsmen and create a market for it in another area.

Lydia was originally from Thyatira (modern day Akhisar, Turkey), one of the greatest areas of commerce in the ancient world. It was a city that was colonized by Alexander after the fall of the Persian empire. Thyatira was known for its various guilds in which people specialized in a trade. One of those guilds was devoted to textiles and the marketing of those textiles. Lydia may have relocated to nearby Phillipi for business advantage or even by personal choice. But there, she had a house that was commodious enough to provide a home for her family and hospitality for others.

By birth, Lydia was a Gentile, but the Bible informs us that she was a believer in the one true God of the Jews (Acts 16:14).

This is evidenced by the fact that on the Sabbath day, Lydia and other women customarily gathered by the riverside to pray. (Because Phillipi was not a Jewish community, there were likely no synagogues there.) Lydia was wise enough to realize that a successful business woman needed to stop her labor for one day to rest, worship God, and rejuvenate.

Paul, Silas, and Timothy encountered Lydia as they were on a journey from Troas to Macedonia. Phillipi was the chief city of Macedonia (Acts 16:12). When they got to Phillipi, they stayed there a few days. On the Sabbath, the three men also retreated to the riverside to worship God. At the riverside, they found Lydia and other women worshipping God already. They began to talk to and worship with the women:

> And on the Sabbath we went out of the city by a river side, where prayer was wont [habitually or by custom] to be made; and we sat down, and spake unto the women which resorted thither.

> And a certain woman named Lydia, a seller of purple, of the city of Thyatira which worshipped God, heard us: whose heart the Lord opened, that she attended unto the things which were spoken of Paul (Acts 16:14).

The King James Version is my preferred translation, however, it provides a limited understanding of the dynamic display of Lydia's wisdom in spiritual matters. Verse 14 says that Lydia "heard" them. One of my favorite Bible writers, Edith Deen[9], interpreted that to mean, perceiving a sound, as in the Greek word, akouō. However my study leads me to conclude that "heard" is probably the Greek word, epakroaomai, which means to "listen attentively to." [10]

This line of reasoning is underscored by another of my favorite translations.[11] Similar to the New King James Version, the verbs are more descriptive.

Translated, the same scripture means, she didn't hear us, but she listened to us, and God caused her to yield careful attention and receive the words of Paul [regarding the gospel of Jesus Christ].

This means that Lydia was a wise woman; she maintained a capacity to be influenced. She had a heart that could be softened by God. Lydia was wise in her own right, but she had the ability to take in new information. Some have a cup that is so full of what they know and believe that new information cannot be added. A woman of Lydia's means could have certainly been dogmatic, maintained a firm stance in her own beliefs, and unwilling to hear the gospel of Jesus Christ. Or, she could have used it as an opportunity for debate.

The second part of the scripture (Acts 16:14) is the key to Lydia's wisdom. She did not rely upon her own knowledge, but that she was sensitive to the prodding of God. This verse reads:

> whose heart the Lord opened, that she attended unto
> the things which were spoken of Paul.

This text verifies our opening premise, that wisdom comes only from God. Because without having a heart that had been opened by God by the Lord, Lydia would not have had the impetus to internalize and receive Paul's message. Lydia not only used good judgment, she also got the understanding. Perhaps then, wisdom (chokmah) causes one to seek a deeper understanding, beyond the superficial. And perhaps the real value of wisdom is not only for the sake of having uncommon knowledge, but for the difference that it will make in your life and the lives of the members of your household.

Indeed, Paul's message made a difference in Lydia's life and in the lives of the members of her household: For after Lydia was baptized, so were all the members of her household. That is the value of wisdom.

Herein lies another significant piece. Lydia is a model for women in business. She had a disposition that caused others to follow her lead in personal and spiritual matters, also. There is sufficient evidence to conclude that Lydia was interpersonally effective and emotionally intelligent.

In a modern context, some leaders resort to a tough, heavy-handed, and sometimes abrasive approach which crushes the spirit of those they are attempting to lead. With the goal of being perceived as capable, no-nonsense business persons, female leaders can easily fall into this trap and, as a result, be deemed ineffective. Because female leadership may come under higher scrutiny, this leadership style may be deemed more harshly when exhibited by female leaders, although abrasiveness is considered to be an undesirable attribute for leaders, notwithstanding gender.

> - accurate, not arrogant
> - direct, not dogmatic
> - firm, not foul
> - to the point, without missing the point of human kindness

A woman of wisdom should therefore consider that it is possible to be direct without being dogmatic; accurate yet not arrogant; business-minded but not boisterous; firm without being foul; and to-the-point without missing the point of human kindness. This is also wisdom.

The Bible informs us that Lydia invited Paul and Silas to her home. Later, in the chapter, the writer [Timothy] recounts the demise of Paul and Silas after they delivered a girl from demon possession. Because this disrupted the economy of the group of men who were selling her services as a fortune teller, Paul and Silas were put into prison. When they were released from prison, they again, returned to the hospitality of Lydia's home in Phillipi.

It is interesting that the city of Phillipi was not unlike many of our cities today. In them, there are women like Lydia who worship the true and living God, but don't yet know Jesus. There are those who rely upon cards and palm readers, fortune tellers, and horoscopes in the manner of ancient women who trusted in the spirits and soothsayers. There are those who have partial truths; who wait to be illuminated by a full gospel message that can minister also to their health and lifestyle needs, as well as to their spiritual and emotional needs. There is a likelihood that there will be modern women who will be like the Biblical prison officer, whose heart was softened by the Lord to receive the gospel that Paul shared with him. Therein is our opportunity to exercise true wisdom—that when the gospel comes to us, we will make room in our hearts to receive it. Pray also for yourself, that you will consistently seek deeper levels of understanding so that you can make a difference in your life and in the lives of the members of your household.

Lydia's wisdom gave rise to the furtherance of the Gospel of Jesus Christ in the city of Phillipi. The small company of believers at Phillipi blossomed into a full ministry that Paul later addressed in his letter to the Phillipians:

> I thank God upon every remembrance of you. For your
> fellowship in the gospel from the first day until now.
>   (Phillipians 1: 3, 5)

Lydia displayed wisdom in her business savvy and in her spiritual discernment (in that she was led by God to embrace the testimony of Jesus). But even greater is the fact that her leadership influence was positive enough that she could lead her household in spiritual matters as well.

Women of Wisdom Walk with God by Presentation and Confirmation

Today's Women of Wisdom must have the clarity of mind to hear God's voice, apply the seven principles listed above to discern true prophets, understand with an uncommon depth, and walk in wisdom.

The Bible says, Thy word is a lamp unto my feet and a light unto my path (Psalm 110:5). We can acknowledge the fact that God's word may sometimes be a lamp to our feet, only. He often does not illuminate the whole journey. More often, God reveals one step at a time, and we have to take the first step in order to see the next one.

We act upon His word by taking the first step. If we are walking as God wills us to walk, it will be confirmed by a sense of harmony, inner peace, and the presentation of the next step. It is sometimes said, "If you take the first step, God will take two." I say this: "When you make a step that is within God's Will, He will confirm it within your spirit and will present the next step. By Confirmation and Presentation—this is a practical description of "how to walk with God."

I must admit that my Christian walk has sometimes been less-than-courageous. In those instances, I failed to boldly move on what I perceived to be a course of action or an opportunity that God might have allowed (His Permissive Will). I both lacked confidence in myself and faith in God. In not wanting to make the wrong decision, I missed some opportunities.

For the most part, however, I have tried to obey God's Expressed Will (The Ten Commandments), but I did not learn until recently to embrace His Permissive Will along with his Expressed Will. Without embracing both, life is a legalistic maze. In some cases, I was like my spiritual forefathers; wanting the security of Egypt and the blessings of Canaan.

You, too might be considering a new ministry or other venture. After you project the needs and ensure the most solid foundation possible, go forth with your ideas and dreams.

Stories like Barak's have helped me to come face-to-face with these truths. Deborah's wisdom has caused me to become more determined to step out on the firm foundation of God's word. By Presentation and Confirmation—that is how I have learned to proceed. I have been most successful when I have gained confidence in my prospective courses of action and those whose counsel I sought by using the checklist at the top of page 148 (expanded version on page 166-168).

Women of Wisdom Use Their Family Resources to Further the Gospel

Priscilla

Priscilla, whom the apostle Paul fondly refers to as "Prisca" in II Timothy 4:19, was a woman of wisdom. She used her resources—her house, her family business, and her partnership with her husband to spread the gospel message of Jesus Christ. As a result, she and her husband were, therefore, instrumental in the furtherance of the gospel in Corinth and in Ephesus.

Priscilla and her husband, Aquila, were tent makers. They worked alongside each other, initially making tents and later, in ministry. Their lives are a template for husbands and wives who desire to become co-laborers in the ministry of the gospel. As husband and wife labor in the cause to teach others about Jesus Christ, they share experiences. The bond between them is strengthened and their love is deepened.

Priscilla and Aquila are mentioned in four books of the New Testament: Acts 18, Romans 16, I Corinthians 16, and II Timothy 4. They first time they were mentioned was when they met Paul, as Paul tarried in Corinth during his second missionary journey. Also a tent maker, Paul readily had something in common with this couple. He stayed at their house in Corinth. He worked in their tent-making business, likely during the week, because the scriptures make the distinction that Paul preached the gospel to the Jews and to the Greeks in the synagogue on the Sabbath Day.

During his stay with them, Paul shared the gospel of Jesus Christ with Priscilla and Aquila. Over one year later, they joined Paul when he travelled from Corinth to Ephesus. As Paul moved on to other cities in the area, Priscilla and Aquila remained in Ephesus. While they were there, a scholarly, well-educated man by the name of Apollos came and began to eloquently preach the message of the one true and living God of the Jews. His message was based on the holy scriptures of the time, which included the baptism of John the Baptist.

In this location, Aquila and Priscilla demonstrated their in-depth understanding of the gospel. Because of their long-time association with Paul and their thorough knowledge of the gospel, Priscilla and Aquila were able to minister to Apollos in Paul's absence. They taught Apollos the full gospel message, privately corrected a few of the errors that he was teaching, and convinced him that Jesus Christ would supersede the anointing of John the Baptist.

Herein lies the crux of Priscilla and Aquila's wisdom and understanding (chokmah and biynah). Chokmah was the wisdom they exercised in making an initial good judgment to befriend the travelling missionary, Paul. In the book of Romans, Priscilla and Aquila are saluted by Paul as his:

> "helpers in Jesus Christ . . . who have for my life laid
> down their own necks . . . ." (Romans 16:3-4)

In order to understand this comment, we must remember that Paul was somewhat of a 'marked man.' People looked at him and remembered him as Saul, who had persecuted Christians. No doubt, when Paul came to Corinth, his reputation preceded him; people were afraid of being imprisoned, scourged, or even stoned to death as Stephen had been. Nevertheless, Priscilla and Aquila took Paul into their home and allowed him to work in their business. What courage that took. Aside from that, it took wisdom: discernment and the ability to judge character.

Next, Priscilla and Aquila got an understanding of the gospel, in a very in-depth manner. It is said, that you don't really know a subject until you teach it. In order to teach Apollos and reason with him on a level to correct his knowledge of the scriptures and convince him, Priscilla and her husband demonstrated that he had not only learned the lessons taught by Paul, but they understood the intricacies of the gospel. Remember that Apollos was a very well-educated man and had been a student of the scriptures for a considerable amount of time. The couple also learned the methods of the gospel ministry—in that they drew Apollos to them privately to correct his errors. They did not challenge him openly or humiliate him by correcting him in the presence of others.

Notice that this mother of wisdom (Priscilla) is never singled out, but is always referred to in conjunction with her husband, Aquila. This establishes the protocol that when partners co-labor in ministry, they are recognized as a unit. The wisdom and understanding that is ascribed to one, is, by association, ascribed to the other. In Corinthians, Paul gives Aquila and Priscilla a final salute "for the church that is in their house." (I Corinthians 16:19).

Women of Wisdom Provide Leadership when they are Heads of Household

The Daughters of Zelophehad Planned for the Future
(Reprinted from *Nothing New Under the Sun*)

The example of women heads of household was given in the Bible. Most women believe the ideal is to have companionship and, perhaps, by co-laboring with a spouse, establish home ownership. But when a woman finds herself alone or chooses to be alone, she must exercise self-reliant leadership in the provision of a home for herself and her dependents.

It is at this time that wisdom is greatly needed. God's will must be consulted every step of the way. We have excellent Biblical examples given to us through the Daughters of Zelophehad and Ruth and Naomi.

As far back as Biblical days, land has been a preferred currency and symbol of wealth and posterity. After Israel worshipped Baal-peor, God sent a plague which slayed 24,000 people. Afterwards, God ordered Moses to take a census. Each tribe was accounted for, as outlined in Numbers 26. Of the original tribe of Manasseh, there were several heirs. However, one descendent from the tribe of Manasseh, (Zelophehad) had five daughters. According to Mosaic Law, daughters could not receive an inheritance of land. Land could only be transferred to sons and Zelophehad had no sons. The courage and conviction of Zelophehad's five daughters resulted in their petition to Moses and Eleazar, the priest. After hearing their case, Moses, by permission of God, granted Zelophehad's daughters a portion of land, an inheritance in Canaan. Their inheritance not only gave them financial security, it sustained the family name. See Numbers 36:11-12.

The daughters' demonstration of perseverance for a noble cause is our example of how to look at the long-range nature of an issue and plan for the future.

Women of Wisdom Engage in Mentoring Relationships

Naomi and Ruth

Ruth, on the advice of her wise mother-in-law Naomi, was able to preserve the land that belonged to their deceased husbands, Mahlon and Elimelech. By showing industry, discretion, and good deportment, Ruth put herself in a position to receive financial favor from Boaz, one of Mahlon's close relatives.

The heart of this story is the relationship that was shared between the two women: one older and wiser; the other younger and malleable. Because she knew the customs of her people, Naomi was able to help her widowed daughter-in-law navigate the subtle nuances of the Jewish culture. Without Naomi's mentorship, Ruth would not have been able to get Boaz to find such favor with her. Naomi's sage advice enabled Ruth to say and to do just the right thing to engender Boaz's help:

14 And Boaz said unto her, At mealtime come thou hither, and eat of the bread, and dip thy morsel in the vinegar. And she sat beside the reapers: and he reached her parched corn, and she did eat, and was sufficed, and left.

15 And when she was risen up to glean, Boaz commanded his young men, saying, Let her glean even among the sheaves, and reproach her not:

16 And let fall also some of the handfuls of purpose for her, and leave them, that she may glean them, and rebuke her not.

17 So she gleaned in the field until even, and beat out that she had gleaned: and it was about an ephah of barley.

18 And she took it up, and went into the city: and her mother in law saw what she had gleaned:
Ruth 2: 14-18

deem her to be a virtuous woman:

6 And she went down unto the floor, and did according to all that her mother in law bade her.

7 And when Boaz had eaten and drunk, and his heart was merry, he went to lie down at the end of the heap of corn: and she came softly, and uncovered his feet, and laid her down.

8 And it came to pass at midnight, that the man was afraid, and turned himself: and, behold, a woman lay at his feet.

9   And he said, Who art thou? And she answered, I am Ruth thine
     handmaid: spread therefore thy skirt over thine handmaid;
     for thou art a near kinsman.

10   And he said, Blessed be thou of the LORD, my daughter: for
     thou hast shewed me more kindness in the latter end than at
     the beginning, inasmuch as thou followedst not young men,
     whether poor or rich.

11   And now, my daughter, fear not; I will do to thee all that thou
     requirest: for all the city of my people doth know that thou
     art a virtuous woman.
     Ruth 3: 6-11

marry her:

13   So Boaz took Ruth, and she was his wife: and when he went
     in unto her, the LORD gave her conception, and she bare a
     son.

14   And the women said unto Naomi, Blessed be the LORD, which
     hath not left thee this day without a kinsman, that his name
     may be famous in Israel.

15   And he shall be unto thee a restorer of thy life, and a nourisher
     of thine old age: for thy daughter in law, which loveth thee,
     which is better to thee than seven sons, hath born him.

16   And Naomi took the child, and laid it in her bosom, and
     became nurse unto it.

17   And the women, her neighbours, gave it a name, saying,
     There is a son born to Naomi; and they called his name Obed:
     he is the father of Jesse, the father of David.

18   Now these are the generations of Pharez: Pharez begat
     Hezron,

19   And Hezron begat Ram, and Ram begat Amminadab,

20 And Amminadab begat Nahshon, and Nahshon begat Salmon

21 And Salmon begat Boaz, and Boaz begat Obed,

22 And Obed begat Jesse, and Jesse begat David.
     Ruth 4:13-22

By the wisdom of these two women, Naomi and Ruth, the seed of
the Messiah was born from their lineage. Further, God restored
milk in Grandmother Naomi's breast so that she could nurse the
baby. Miracle upon miracle happened because of their wisdom
and their faithfulness.

If you are an older and wiser woman, do take a younger woman
under your wing and teach her the things that will help her to
raise her children, keep her family intact, handle her finances,
or manage the multiple demands of a career. In turn, you will be
blessed and the younger woman's life will be enriched. She will
not have to learn everything by trial and error.

Certainly Ruth, Naomi, and the daughters of Zelophehad could
be grouped among the virtuous women of the Bible. The text
which refers to King Lemuel's mother could also be applied to
them. It is found in Proverbs 31:15:

>   She eyeth a field and purchaseth it, with the fruit
> of her hands she planteth a vineyard. (Proverbs 31:16)

Relationship Status of the Bible's Women of Wisdom

	Era	Married	Presumed Single	Widowed	Evidence of Wisdom
Deborah	Old Testament	x			Guided Barak in Battle
Miriam	Old Testament		x		Secured a nurse for the Baby Moses, which was his own biological mother, Jochabed. Was a leader among the Hebrew Women; a prophetess also.
Anna	New Testament		x	x	Served God with prayers and fastings and spake of Christ to all who were in a position to seek Him.
Daughters of Philip	New Testament		x		They were virgins: their lives were in harmony with God's principles and they did prophesy.

	Era	Married	Presumed Single	Widowed	Evidence of Wisdom
Huldah	Old Testament	x			Prophesied that Josiah would not see God's pronouncement of evil upon Jerusalem.
Lydia	New Testament		x		A business woman who led her family financially and spiritually; her entire household was baptized as a result of her influence.
Priscilla	New Testament	x			Opened up her home to the apostle Paul for "cottage" meetings; taught Apollos the full gospel message.
Daughters of Zelophehad	Old Testament		x		Sought property ownership in order to preserve their inheritance.
Naomi	Old Testament			x	Counseled her daughter-in-law regarding how best to gain favor from Boaz, a wealthy kinsman.
Ruth	Old Testament			x	Accepted the counsel of her mother-in-law regarding how to find favor while residing in a foreign land.

Something Extra . . . .

Women of Wisdom can discern True Prophets and Prophetesses

Throughout her life, a woman will hear the spoken word of many persons. She must have a way by which to measure true messengers from false ones. Seven principles of a true prophetess were given on page 148. Here they are listed again, along with the scriptural references which support each of the seven principles. The research for this section was compiled by my own mother of wisdom, the late Josephine L. Ridley:

Prophets and Prophetesses:

1. Must uphold the Law

> If any man thinks himself to be a prophet, or spiritual, let him acknowledge the things I write unto you are the Commandments of the Lord. (I Corinthians 14: 37)

> To the law and to the testimony if they speak not according to these, there is no truth in them (Isaiah 8:20).

> Remember Hananiah's false claim that the Judeans' Baylonian captivity would only last for two years. God said that it would last for seventy years. Hananiah was punished and died for making the people trust in a lie. (Jeremiah 28:15)

2. Must keep pagan practices separate from the doctrines of Christianity[13]

> 8 . . . that woman Jezebel, which called herself a prophetess, to teach and seduce my servants to commit fornication and to eat food being sacrificed

unto idols . . . did not repent of her fornications. (Revelation 2:20-21)

3. Must be repentant of one's own sins and disciplined appropriately

> . . . and Aaron looked upon Miriam, and behold, she was leprous. I beseech thee, lay not the sin upon us, wherein we have done foolishly, and wherein we have sinned . . . let her be shut out from the camp seven days, and after that let her be received in again. And Miriam was shut out from the camp seven days: and the people journeyed not until Miriam was brought in again . . . (Numbers 12: 11-15)

4. Must be of good moral reputation

> . . . Anna, a prophetess . . . of the tribe of Aser, [was a virgin who married and lived with a man seven years until he died.] And she was a widow . . . which departed not from the temple, but served God with fastings and prayers . . . and spake of him, Christ, to all that looked for redemption. (Luke 2:36-38, paraphrased)

> Philip, the evangelist . . . had four daughters, virgins, which did prophesy (Acts 21: 8-9)

5. Must recognize Jesus Christ as Savior and soon-coming King

> Beloved, believe not every spirit, but try the spirits whether they are of God; because many false prophets are gone out into the world. Hereby know ye the Spirit of God: every Spirit that confesseth that Jesus Christ is come in the flesh is of God. And every Spirit that confesseth not that Jesus Christ is come in the flesh is not of God . . . . and this is that spirit of antichrist (I John 4: 1-4).

6. Must crucify self, ensuring that their prophecies yield to the word of God and the teachings of Christ and not to their own doctrines

Set thy face against the daughters of the people, which prophesy out of their own heart; and prophesy thou against them. (Ezekiel 13:17)

Thus saith the Lord God: Woe unto the foolish prophets that follow their own spirit and have seen nothing! (Ezekiel 13: 3)

7. Must foretell things that actually come to pass

Hilkah, the high priest . . . went unto Huldah, the prophetess, the wife of Shallum . . . She dwelt in Jerusalem in the college; and they communed with her. And she said, Thus saith the Lord . . . . [to King Josiah] . . . . thine eyes shall not see all the evil which I will bring upon this place . . . . (II Kings 22:14,20)

{Note: the capture of Jerusalem by the Babylonian King, Nebuchadnezzar happened after Josiah's death, during the reign of his second son, Eliakim (renamed Jehoiakim). This fulfilled Huldah's prophecy. (II Chronicles 36:4-7).}

8. Must present a message that reinforces what God has told you to do

False prophetess Noadiah according to Nehemiah was one of those who came to him to put him in fear so that he, Nehemiah, would not finish rebuilding the wall as God had instructed him to. (Read Nehemiah 6: 14 in a modern translation).

True prophetess Deborah said to Barak, "hath not the Lord God of Israel commanded thee, saying, Go, and draw toward Mount Tabor, and take with thee 10,000 men of the children of Naphtali, and of the children of Zebulun?"

BIBLE PROMISE FOR YOU

"To the law and to the testimony: if they speak not according to this word, it is because there is no light in them."

Isaiah 8:20

Making it Practical
Guidelines for Walking in "Presentation and Confirmation"

Once my husband and I hiked down to the base of the natural falls at Fall Creek Falls State Park near Cookeville, Tennessee (USA). Getting to the bottom of this fall required us to descend nearly 300 feet from the roadside. Our descent was fairly easy and quite enjoyable. At the bottom, the mist was cool and refreshing.

However, looking upward to the roadside from the base of the fall made a safe return seem nearly impossible. There, at the base of the fall, I learned a useful lesson that has a meaningful spiritual application. The ascent to the top is characterized by rocky ledges unpredictably interspersed with patches of soft mud. I noted that by stepping from rock to rock, the daunting task of ascending could be accomplished.

On life's journey, look for your first sure step. Consider that to be 'Presentation.' If you are able to make that step, firmly, comfortably, that's Confirmation. Quite miraculously, the next step will appear. That is Presentation. Make it. Confirmation. Presentation and confirmation; making one confirmed step at a time. That's how life's difficult paths are navigated.

What evidence of "Presentation and Confirmation" has God given to you in the past?

_____

_____

What Difficult Path Are You Facing Today?

_____

_____

Write your spiritual uncertainty here:

_____

_____

Presentation

What advice has been given to you?

What sure step is at-hand? . . . . What option are you considering?

_____

_____

Confirmation

Test the advice, the advice-giver, or the option as follows:

- Does it uphold the Ten-Commandment Law?
- Is the option free from immoral practices?
- Is the option supported by the doctrines of Christianity?
- Does the option reinforce the word of God (the Bible) and the teachings of Christ?

If so, make this step. The next one will be presented. Again, confirm your planned step by asking yourself the questions above. If it passes the test, go ahead and make that step. The next step will be presented.

Female Leadership

Like Lydia, the most successful and balanced businesswomen
will be able to engender others to themselves and influence
them. Achieved through a combination of competence paired
with a woman's inherent qualities, this version of leadership is
natural and far superior to a female version of command and
control models that emanate from classical leadership theory
(Great Man, Trait, Machiavellian, etc.). By studying the lives of
Deborah, Miriam, Lydia, and other women of the Bible, today's
women may be able to glean fresh ideas and principles for leading
that are gender-specific and fit a wider range of contemporary
leadership scenarios and expectations.

ENDNOTES

1   At the time of this writing, Hillary Rhodham-Clinton was Senator of New York and Prime Minister Margaret Thatcher was living. By the time of publication, Mrs. Clinton had waged an impressive bid for the Democratic Nomination for President of the United States and was serving as Secretary of State under President, Barack Obama.

2   Harriet Tubman is said to have been an informant for the Union troops in the United States Civil War, primarily due to her knowledge of the "underground" geography between the southern states and the northern states of America.

3   Condoleeza Rice was named the National Security Advisor for George H. W. Bush. She garnered this post because of her study of international policy and politics, especially of the Soviet Union and Czechoslovakia.

4   Humorous comment: Deborah was a model for modern career woman. She had an outdoor office, underneath the palm trees.

5   *Webster's* Collegiate Dictionary

6   To discomfit means to frustrate or confuse.

7   The definition of "buckler" was found via "Google" Search in the Wikipedia Online Encyclopedia.

8   Moses was married to Zipporah, the daughter of Jethro. Jethro was married to Jael.

9   The information about Mollusks and the purple dye secreted by them were found at:
http://www.internationalstandardbible.com/D/dye-dyeing.html
http://books.google.com/books?id=5-6aK3QtkQYC&pg=PA114
&lpg=PA114&dq=purple+dye+in+the+bible&source=bl&ots=K
JTpahPClf&sig=qhI-az1iwXML72R4JOd5Czmgc_o&hl=en&ei=0
Dj_SunNIpCDnQefucH0Bg&sa=X&oi=book_result&ct=result&res

num=7&ved=0CBkQ6AEwBg#v=onepage&q=purple%20dye%20
in%20the%20bible&f=false

http://pffc-online.com/mag/paper_history_shellfish_royalty/

10   Deen, Edith, *All of the Women of the Bible*, page 224.

11   Comparatively, the King James translators use the word, "heard",
      again eleven verses later in Acts 16:25 when referring to the
      prisoners, and at midnight Paul and Silas prayed, and sang praises
      unto God: and the prisoners heard them."

      What meaning would you infer about the word, "heard" as used in
      this passage of scripture?

12   *La Sainte Bible, Ancien et Nouveau Testament; traduite de l'hebrēu
      et du grec en français courant. 1997. Nouvelle édition révisée.*
      Villiers-le-Bel: Alliance Biblique Universelle.

13   *Vine's Expository Dictionary* defined fornication as the Greek
      word, "porneia." Fornication in Revelation 2:20-21, referred to
      Jezebel's deeds, both literally and metaphorically. The literal or
      actual meaning of fornication is illicit sex. The metaphorical or
      symbolic meaning of fornication refers to illicit activities in the
      Christian church, mixing pagan practices like Baal worship with
      the Christian doctrines and practices. In Revelation 2:20-21, Jesus,
      through John on the island of Patmos, condemns the Church of
      Thyatira for embracing the spirit of Jezebel.

REFERENCES

Deen, Edith. 1955. *All the Women of the Bible*. New York: Harper & Row.

La Sainte Bible, Ancien et Nouveau Testament; traduite de l'hebrēu et du grec en français courant. 1997. Nouvelle édition révisée. Villiers-le-Bel: Alliance Biblique Universelle.

Ridley, Josephine L. Ridley. 2000. Personal Study Notes entitled, "Prophets and Prophetesses," unpublished. The section on prophetesses was developed from the study notes of my own mother of wisdom, the beloved Josephine Louise Parham Ridley.

Smith, Constance Ridley. 2002. *Nothing New Under the Sun: Lessons on Living from Women of the Bible*. Hamilton: Breakthrough Communications.

The Holy Bible Authorized King James Version (KJV), Crown Reference Edition, 1985. Nashville: Holman Bible Publishers.

Vine,W.E., Unger, Merrill F. and William White, Jr. 1985. *Vine's Expository Dictionary of the Bible*. Nashville: Thomas Nelson, Inc.

Online Sources:
http://www.biblestudytools.com/OnlineStudyBible/bible.cgi?word=Ruth+3&section=0&version=kjv&new=1&oq=&NavBook=ru&NavGo=3&NavLastChapter=%3E|&NavCurrentChapter=3

www.answers.com/topic/condoleezza-rice

en.wikipedia.org/wiki/Condoleezza_Rice

http://www.biblegateway.com/kcyword/index.php?search=wi
sdom&version1=9&searchtype=all&startnumber=26&start
number=126&startnumber=201

http://www.biblestudytools.com/Lexicons/Hebrew/heb.cgi?n
umber=02451&version=kjv#Legend

Joy

What is joy? There are so many interpretations of the words "happiness" and "joy" that we may find it hard to distinguish one person's interpretation from another's. It is even possible that we unknowingly confuse the earthly concept of happiness with the biblical concept of joy. Those in my social media network generally agree that happiness may indeed come from circumstances, but joy is a state of being that transcends circumstances.

What is the source of joy? How can you get it? How can you keep it?

In this chapter we will:

1   Distinguish among the several biblical words that are used for the English word, joy.
2   Examine the lives of several women in the New Testament who found joy.
3   Find out what these Women of Joy had in common.

Women of Joy
Find joy in service

For every God-given principle there is a counterfeit. When misguided, human beings develop inferior, second-rate concepts of biblical truths. Such inferior concepts fall beneath God's ideal for His people. The truth about joy and happiness is no exception.

The American Declaration of Independence refers to the right of every man to have "life, liberty, and [engage in] the pursuit of happiness." In this case, young Thomas Jefferson used the word "happiness" to refer to material gain, property rights, and self-governance. The colonists sought to be regarded as equal beings who possessed thinking abilities and rational properties that were equal to those of Great Britain's King George III[1]. By this line of thought, they established their qualification to rule based on merit (their abilities), rather than having such qualification to be based upon birthright (the British monarchy). The Declaration established that the American colonies met the criteria to be self-governing. It also affirmed that each man had the right to live, be free, and pursue his own goals. For those who signed the Declaration of Independence, happiness was all about what independent men, rugged individualists, could carve out of life for themselves.

This concept of "happiness" is vastly different from what the biblical concept of happiness infers. Biblical happiness is more accurately viewed as a Declaration of Interdependence because the women in our study who found happiness (translated as "joy") were in pursuit of corporate, rather than individual, goals. They lived lives that were engaged in service to others. Those women are Rhoda, Anna, and the women who were at the tomb of Jesus. Each of these women showed an abiding concern about the happiness and well-being—not of self, but of others.

Confused about the essence of happiness, I once asked a wise gentleman,

"Mr. Carter, What is happiness?"

"There is no such thing as happiness," he replied. "But there is contentment. Contentment resembles happiness."

Without having the luxury to design perfect circumstances, we sometimes struggle to find such contentment —wholeness, alignment, and inner peace. Perhaps the struggle exists because we often confuse the earthly concept of happiness (which was articulated by Thomas Jefferson) with the biblical concept of happiness.

Joy trumps life's circumstances. That statement rings truth in the lives of women of the Bible who had joy. I also found that these biblical women had three things in common. The first thing that the three Women of Joy shared in common was a life of service. They were not without the material comforts that they needed, but they did not have an inflated concern over material worth. Perhaps they knew the Bible principle which states, [S]h e that loves silver shall not be satisfied with silver; nor [s]he that loves abundance with increase: this, too, is vanity" (Ecclesiastes 5:10). Each woman had material provisions, but each built her legacy on something much more lasting—service to others. Anna ministered in the temple day and night; Rhoda served as doorkeeper in the household of Mary Mark; and the women at the tomb of Jesus were planning to anoint the body of the crucified Christ with sweet spices. Each attained joy while they were engaged in active service in a cause that was greater than their own material needs.

The second thing that these women had in common was that each was searching for something. Anna was looking for the Messiah, Rhoda was looking for the release of Peter from Herod's prison, and the women came to the tomb looking for the body of the crucified Christ. The Bible tells us that each woman experienced joy at the end of her search—when she received the answer to her heartfelt desire or prayer. To understand their expressions of joy it is helpful to understand the critical essence of what each woman was looking for. To increase our understanding, we can turn to the parable of a woman who rejoiced, the woman who found her lost coin in Luke 15: 8. We take the liberty to consider this parable in conjunction with the three women who experienced joy because in this passage of scripture, the word translated as "rejoiced" is the biblical word "chairō," which is quite similar to "chara," a biblical word which is translated as gladness or joy. These words will be discussed later. The parable of the woman with the lost coin accompanies the parables of the shepherd who lost one of his 100 sheep and the man who lost the prodigal son. These parables, but specifically the one about the woman who searched for the lost coin, provide the central theme of application for today's woman who is searching for joy. That theme is to apply her mission of service in working to recover souls that are lost. In Luke 15:8, the parable prescribes the methodology for searching for that which is lost:

1. Light a candle
2. Sweep the house
3. Seek diligently

Seeking, according to Strong's [G2212] is the Greek word, zēteō, which means "to seek [in order to find out] by thinking, meditating, reasoning; or to enquire into or to seek after, seek for, aim at, strive after." This can also be our method for seeking temporal pursuits like education, life's comforts, and civil liberties such as those that Thomas Jefferson indicated, but more so, like Rhoda, Anna, and the women who were at the tomb of Jesus, this is how we must approach our ministry in recovering that or those who are lost.

The third thing that each of these women had in common was that they experienced "chara," which is a particular type of joy. "Chara" is used frequently in the New Testament. According to Vine (1984), *chara* is joy that is caused by an occasion or circumstance, such as the answer to heartfelt prayer or relief from trying circumstances. "Chara," is the type of joy that comes as a result of receiving something that has been long-awaited,—talked about, and—prayed about; or seeing good triumph (win) over evil. Rhoda, Anna, and the women at the tomb of Jesus had life experiences that were culminated in their expressions of "chara" joy.

Chara is different from other biblical words for joy that are explained also by Vine:

> *Tuv*—which is being joyful over material things and one's portion of goods

> *Simchah*—mirth and gaiety such as that which is caused by pleasure

> *Chedvah*—which is simple joy

> *Rinnah*—is a shout of proclamation, praise, or supplication; joy that comes in the morning after weeping has endured for a night (Psalm 30:5).

From the stories of these women (Rhoda, Anna, and the women at the tomb of Christ) we can derive the gist of joy, which is the search, the service, and the answer to prayer. We will find that in the middle, between one's search and one's answer to prayer is the pathway called service. For the woman of today, this indicates that each of us has access to joy not as we wait on the sidelines, wishing and praying, but as we are also serving the

"Chara" Joy comes as a result of:

Search
> ➤ looking for what has been lost or bound

Service
> ➤ working for a cause

Answer to Prayer
> ➤ receiving something that has been looked for, long-awaited, -talked about, and -prayed about.

> ➤ seeing good triumph (win) over evil.

needs of humanity and as we are searching for holy outcomes to our hopes, dreams, ambitions, and life issues. The apex of our service is working to bring lost souls into oneness with their Creator and Savior. Feature that, finding your own joy while doing for others— deriving fulfilment and pleasure from performing acts of kindness or missions. It's hard to imagine. Due to the incidence of human cruelty and the connotations that are generally associated with the position of servants in many places in the world (including America), many people have bought into the belief that servant status is not something to which they should aspire.

In most cases, serving is deemed something to be ashamed of. However, in the work of the gospel, we need not be ashamed of providing service to others and being the hands and feet of the gospel message. Lives will be transformed for Christ by our "conversation," which is, our manner of life, our deportment , and what we do, rather than what we say. In New Testament scripture, the word "conversation" is generally the Greek word "anastrophe," which refers to one's actions, not one's words.

Read the following scriptures with this in mind:

" . . . but be thou an example of the believers, in word, in conversation, in charity, in spirit, in faith, in purity." I Timothy 4:11-14

> Service should not be confused with servitude.

"Having your conversation honest among the Gentiles: that, whereas they speak against you as evildoers, they may by your good works, which they shall behold, glorify God in the day of visitation." I Peter 2: 12

"Likewise, ye wives, be in subjection to your own husbands; that, if any obey not the word, they also may without the word be won by the conversation of the wives;" I Peter 3:1

Therefore, we have no need to be ashamed of being a servant in the cause of the gospel message. "Service should not be confused with servitude."

In my own personal search for joy, Vine's *Expository Dictionary of Biblical Words* clarified the path to joy:

"Joy is associated with life . . . Experiences of sorrow prepare for, and enlarge, the capacity for joy" (1985 p. 335). That passage provided a "wow" moment for me. I began to look for joy on the horizon, for I had certainly had my experiences of sorrow. Perhaps, in the absence of peace, alignment, and fulfillment, I was being *prepared* to receive joy.

Perhaps, I thought, one's capacity to receive joy is proportionate to the gulf that is created by the lack of joy. I began to consider that one's capacity to receive joy may be conditioned or *prepared* in much the same way that the big fish was *prepared* to swallow Jonah in its mouth.

A fish's mouth is not ordinarily large enough to swallow a man whole, but the Bible states:

> "And God prepared a great fish to swallow up Jonah."
> Jonah 1:17

Loss, calamity, betrayal, and misunderstandings surrounded me and thereby clouded my perception of happiness, but they also created the conditions for my joy. God *prepared* me to receive joy. I recited the Bible promise found in Colossians 3:2: "Set your affection on things above, not on things on the earth" and life took on new meaning. When I did that, I found that my true joy, what really made me happy was using my skills, gifts, and talents to provide service to others. That is who I naturally am. That is who I, by my upbringing , was conditioned to be. That is where I, like Rhoda, Anna, and the biblical Women at the Tomb of Jesus Christ have found joy. In my work of service, God provided answers to my heartfelt prayers and gave me the desires of my heart. I took care of His business and He took care of mine. Yet, I got the better end of the deal.

Through the work of service, I experienced "chara" joy. Let us now examine the lives of each Biblical women who also found "chara" joy.

Rhoda

The Bible describes Rhoda as a damsel. In this case, the word "damsel" indicates that Rhoda was a maid and doorkeeper in the house of those who employed her. Rhoda's story is revealed in but a few verses of the Bible (Acts 12:12-17), but her place in Bible history speaks volumes and is valuable to women today. Rhoda wasn't a queen, she was a maid; not a judge, but a doorkeeper; not a teacher, evangelist, nor wife of a noble man. Rhoda was simply, a servant. So what can we learn from her? What can *she* teach us?

Rhoda's message is the message of finding joy in service. Rhoda is one of few Biblical characters recorded by the Bible as having joy or gladness due to circumstances that happened around her, though not necessarily *for* her. Fathom that. As women, we are often looking for someone to make us happy, give us the things that we want out of life, and "complete our package." Rhoda was joyful in her position of service: as a doorkeeper; as a prayer partner; as a bearer of good news; and as a witness to God's goodness in the lives of others.

When the prayers of those she served were answered, she, too, was joyful. The type of joy that Rhoda experienced is the Greek word "*chara*." Rhoda found *chara*, joy which is caused by an occasion of joy, in this case, the answer to prayer. Rhoda's story comes to us in Acts Chapter 12.

Rhoda's moment of joy is nestled within the story of the disciple, Peter, who had been sent to prison by Herod Agrippa.2 Prior to the time of this story, Herod had executed the disciple James. He was holding Peter in prison until after Easter. At that time, Herod would execute his plan to kill Peter, also. Acts Chapter 12, verse 5 lets us know that Peter's friends were gathered at the home of Mary Mark,[3] praying on his behalf. Rhoda was the doorkeeper at the residence.

As a result of their intercessory prayer, Peter miraculously escaped from a double set of soldiers, two of which were chained to him to prevent Peter's movement without their knowledge. Yet, by the power of an angel, the chains fell off of his hands and Peter walked past both sets of soldiers without being detected. An angel escorted Peter from the prison to the street of the city. Peter walked the rest of the journey alone and arrived at the house of Mary Mark, where intercessory prayer was being offered on his behalf. Rhoda was the first person to see Peter after his escape. Rhoda experienced joy when she recognized Peter standing at the door.

Although she was a servant, Rhoda was in tune with and supportive of the goals and activities of the household. In addition to performing the job, her heart was aligned with what her employer wanted and valued for the scripture indicates, during very late hours at night, when most were sleeping, or at least, sleepy, Rhoda was alert enough to perform her job and accurately recognize the voice of Peter. She quickly ran to get others who were praying for Peter at that very moment. It would have been quite easy for Rhoda to be indifferent to the season of prayer that was important to her mistress and those who were in her mistress's company, but she found joy in her humble position of service.

Chara joy makes you excel in whatever position you find yourself and brighten the corner where you are

When I was between the ages of 8 and 12, my mother often said to me, "Constance, be a task great or small, do it well or not at all." In my mind, only, I would say, "Not at all." Even though

I made mental protests by internalizing the words "not at all," mama's charge was prophetic and set the course for my life. As a result, I've always tried to make lemonade out of a lemon, excel at sometimes impossible tasks and situations, keep objects past their apparent usefulness, and maintain hope in situations that others find hopeless. Perhaps Rhoda had received similar training from her mother. It would have been quite easy for Rhoda to be indifferent to the season of prayer that was important to her mistress and those who were in her mistress's company. After all, she was just a doorkeeper. Yet, this was not the case with Rhoda.

Chara joy causes you to run and tell others.

When Peter arrived at the house, he knocked on the door and Rhoda, answered the door. Hearing and recognizing his voice, she was so full of gladness (*chara* joy) that she forgot to let Peter in:

14And when she knew Peter's voice, [Rhoda] opened not the gate for gladness, but ran in, and told how Peter stood before the gate.

> When the King of Joy knocks on the door of your heart, don't forget to open it and invite him in.

The original word that was translated as "gladness" in Acts 12:14 is "*chara*." The transcribers of the King James Version saw the word "chara," but in this passage of scripture, they used the English word "gladness." However, "chara" is usually translated by the transcribers as "joy" in other instances where it appears in the New Testament. Therefore, in this scriptural reference, the words gladness and joy are interchangeable. Rhoda's gladness matches Vine's three definitions of "chara,"

1)an occasion that one recognizes to be valuable; 2)something good that has happened, or; 3) the fact that someone of worth has appeared. "Chara" joy is also experienced when persons see that good has triumphed over evil. The latter type of "chara" joy was demonstrated by the women who went to the tomb of Jesus Christ.

The Women at the Tomb of Christ

(Mary Magdalene, Mary, the mother of James, Salome, Joanna, and others)

The story about the women at the empty tomb is recorded by all four of the gospel writers, Matthew, Mark, Luke, and John. Each writer contributes a different perspective on the events that happened. Many Bible critics get 'hung up' on the variation in the written accounts, but when the emphasis is placed on the commonalities in their accounts, the value in the story of the women at the tomb appears. One of the criticisms is that each writer of the gospel varies in his listing of which women were present at the tomb,

Writer of the Gospel	Names of Women at the Empty Tomb
Matthew (Matthew 28:1)	Mary Magdalene and the other Mary
Mark (Mark 16:1)	Mary Magdalene, Mary, the mother of James, and Salome
Luke (Luke 24:10)	Mary Magdalene, Mary, the mother of James, Joanna, and other women
John (John 20:1)	Mary Magdalene

Each woman who was named was either an eyewitness to the miracles of Christ or had experienced the goodness and virtue of Jesus Christ during His ministry. While each gospel writer varies in whom was named, all four include Mary Magdalene in their listings. They were all familiar with Mary Magdalene. He had healed her and others that she knew. She could, therefore, attest to the goodness of His ministry. She was there when He was crucified, scourged, and buried (Mark 15: 40-41; Mark 16:9) and now she is also found returning to the tomb of Jesus to anoint his body. Mary Magdalene, therefore, has a primary role among the women at the tomb and in our understanding of "chara" joy.

Our understanding of the fourth condition of "chara" joy (seeing good triumph over evil) is enhanced from Mary Magdalene's presence and her perspective because her life was once characterized by evil, having been afflicted by seven devils before Christ healed and delivered her. Her reaction to the empty tomb appropriately personifies joy in good triumphing over evil. No woman in the Bible felt more grateful to Christ than Mary Magdalene, out of whom he drove seven devils. Despite her past, Mary Magdalene was healed by the virtue of Christ and delivered to perform the ministry of coming to anoint the buried body of Christ with sweet spices. The empty tomb was a marvellous testimony to the triumph of good over evil.

Chara joy compels you to change your course of action and tell others about your joy

The women came to the tomb to bring sweet spices to anoint the body of Christ. Like Rhoda, when they experienced chara joy (seeing an empty tomb), they ran to tell others. According to Matthew's account of the story, by the time that Mary and Mary Magdalene came to see the sepulchre, a great earthquake from heaven had ushered in an angel who had rolled the stone away from the entrance to the sepulchre. As they approached the sepulchre, they saw the angel sitting on the stone. In verse 6, the angel informed the two Marys that "He is not here, for He is risen . . ." He bid them to go away quickly from the sepulchre to tell the disciples that Christ had risen. Verse 8 confirms that the two women left the empty tomb with fear and great joy *(chara)*;

and did run to bring His disciples the message that Christ had risen just as he said that he would. (Matthew 28:1-8)

This is similar to what happened when Rhoda saw Peter standing at the gate. Gladness filled her heart; so much so that she forgot to unlatch the gate and let him in the house. She ran to tell others. Like Rhoda, the chara joy experienced by the two Marys in Matthew 28:8 caused them to obey the angel and run to inform the disciples about it.

The women were bidden by the angel to go and tell others that Christ had arisen and that the tomb was empty. It is no coincidence that these women—the two Marys—foreshadowed Christian evangelism. Mary Magdalene and the other Mary were first to fulfill the gospel commission that was later given by Jesus Christ, which is recorded later in the same chapter of Matthew 28:19-20, "Go ye therefore and teach all nations . . . ."

This was also true about the wise men who spotted the star, afar, in the East at the birth of Christ. They followed it until they found the location of the Christ child. Matthew 2:10 records, "When they saw the star, they rejoiced with exceeding great [you guessed it—chara] joy." When they had given thanks for the Christ child, they gave gifts of gold, frankincense and myrrh, then left to return to their own country, no doubt, telling others.

As with the previous aspects of joy, service and the search, this aspect also has implications for today's woman. That is, when you have received the answer to prayer, witness to someone else about the faithfulness of God in your life's experience.

Chara is the type of joy that makes you treasure and protect it.

Jesus told a parable which compared the kingdom of heaven to a treasure hidden in the field. When the man finds it, he values it so much that he hides the treasure so that no one else will find it, then he goes to sell all he has so that he can buy the field (Matthew 13:44).

Faithfulness to God's calling on your life brings chara joy

Christ told another parable that ends in *chara* joy, the parable of the talents. To the man who received five talents from his master, invested it, and gained five others, Christ said, "Well done, thou good and faithful servant; thou hast been faithful over a few things, I will make thee ruler over many things; enter into the joy (*chara*) of thy lord.

The Bible examples are clear: engaging in service allows a person to find something bigger than "oneself" to focus upon. Ironically, by spending less time on self-serving pursuits and opting, instead, to serve others, one's influence is enlarged. Spending less time on "self" does not diminish a woman. It augments her.

> Spending less time on "self" does not diminish a woman. It augments her.

This was also true about the final woman of joy to be discussed, Anna, the prophetess.

Anna

Anna, whose name means grace, was a widow in her 80s. She had been a widow for most of her life. The Bible says, in Luke 2:36-38:

36 And there was one Anna, a prophetess, the daughter of Phanuel, of the tribe of Aser: she was of a great age, and had lived with an husband seven years from her virginity;

37 And she was a widow of about four score and four years which departed not from the temple, but served God with fastings and prayers night and day.

38 And she coming in that instant, gave thanks likewise unto the Lord, and spake of him to all of them that looked for redemption in Jerusalem.

It would have been easy for Anna to be discouraged after seven short-lived years of wedded bliss, living with a husband. As a young widow she could have remarried. That was certainly an option that was available to her by custom (Read I Corinthians 7:8-9 and Ephesians and I Timothy 5:9, 14). Or, she could have become like the unseemly widows described in scripture:

"and withal they learn to be idle, wandering about from house to house; not only idle, but tattlers also, and busybodies, speaking things which they ought not." I Timothy 5:11-13

Instead Anna was a godly woman, whose life fits this description which was given by Timothy, "a widow indeed, and desolate, trusted in God, and continue with supplications and prayers night and day." (I Timothy 5: 5).

Anna followed the faith of her upbringing and looked for the Messiah. As a prophetess, Anna had dedicated her life to proclaiming the hope of the Messiah's appearing. Some incorrectly argue that Anna was not a prophet on her own merit (Clarke and Barnes, online) by stating that at the time Anna lived, prophecy had ceased—or that perhaps she was called a prophetess because her husband had been a prophet.

However, if it is true that people would rather see a sermon than to hear one, Anna's life and actions in the temple, fasting night and day, pointed to her belief that the One who would redeem Israel would come. When Christ was born, Mary and Joseph brought Him to the temple in Jerusalem. When Anna saw Him, she gave thanks and began to go and inform others that the hope and consolation of Israel had appeared. This was a moment of *chara* joy for Anna. What she had dedicated her life to had finally arrived. The promise made by prophets such as Ezekiel were now manifest. Anna *acted* in accordance with the prophecy. Those who observed her knew that she believed that the Messiah would come. Anna's faithfulness in service gave her the joy needed to sustain even after Christ had been crucified.

As a daughter of the tribe of Aser or Asher (Luke 2:36), Anna knew her place in the inheritance for God's people. (Ezekiel 33:24). In fact, the meaning of the word Asher is "happiness."

Chara joy is a promise which comes from obedience and service to God.

Set the parameters for your joy on things that are likely to be accomplishable. If you are attaching your happiness on a person, a temporal situation (which is governed by the ebbs and flows of the life cycle or the economy) or an elusive state of conditions that it is not probable that you will attain, you will remain without joy. However, when you love the things that God also loves and adopt the mind of Christ, your joy will be full.

In ministry:

And the seventy returned again with joy, saying, Lord, even the devils are subject unto us through thy name.

In His provision and plan for your life:

About the birth of John the Baptist, the angel Gabriel predicted to Zacharias, a troubled and fearful father-to be, "And thou shalt have joy *(chara)* and gladness and many shall rejoice at his birth" (Luke 1:14).

This, in fact, did come to pass (Read Luke 1:58)

In your attitude toward sin:

"Likewise, I say unto you, there is joy in the presence of the angels of God over one sinner that repenteth" (Luke 15:10).

As you seek to overcome life's temptations:

"The joy of the Lord is my strength" (Nehemiah 8:10).

May you and I remain faithful in the Lord's service, for that is true joy.

BIBLE PROMISE FOR YOU

This book of the law shall not depart out of thy mouth; but thou shalt meditate therein day and night, that thou mayest observe to do according to all that is written therein: for then thou shalt make thy way prosperous, and then thou shalt have good success (Joshua 1:8).

Summary

A woman who finds "chara" will be one who is actively engaged in service. Indeed, this is one of life's ironies. The immediate benefits of service help those in need, however, the ultimate benefit of service helps the ones who serve . . . to keep their minds on something other than themselves and the void, empty spaces in their own lives, the proverbial "lost coins" that we may be seeking. The stories of Rhoda, Anna, and the women at the tomb of Jesus demonstrate this type of joy. Each Bible story shows us that these Women of Joy were "doers," not hearers only, of the gospel. Collectively, their stories show us what joy is and how to engage oneself while waiting for an answer to prayer. The questions that we, today's women, should ask ourselves are, "Where can I best find my place in service?" "How can I be a doer of the gospel?" "What do I have to give that is needed by humanity?"

"Chara" joy is the reaction that a woman experiences when she receives what she has, for a long time, been praying for. Chara joy is also what a woman feels when she witnesses a triumphant conclusion of good over the forces of evil. Chara is the joyful relief from a bad situation. "What are you now seeking? What are you earnestly praying for? Over what injustice are you anticipating that good will triumph?" These are your lost coins; the answers to these questions frame your personal search. When you have reclaimed these coins, you will likely find the joy that you may feel is missing from your life.

Even more important to God than our service and our search, is what we are searching for. God is looking for a transformation in our thinking. He wants to be the object of that search. He wants us to desire a deeper relationship with Him and have the expectancy of our Lord's soon-coming near to our hearts, even more fervently than the temporal things that we desire and pray for. He wants to be our lost coin. As such, we must seek Jesus as ardently as we seek our material comforts and earthly possessions. We must look for the Messiah as earnestly as the widow Anna did, despite the loss that she had experienced in her personal life. We must pray for those who are in bondage to their circumstances, even as Rhoda's prayer partners prayed for Peter's release from prison chains. Like the women at the tomb, we must serve needs and go on God's errands, even as we pray for good to triumph over evil. God hears our prayers. As He answers them according to His will, we will not always be happy, but as we minister to others in God's service, we will have lasting joy.

As for our material comforts, when we take care of God's business, He is faithful to take care of our needs. My life is a living testimony of God's faithfulness in this regard. The words of songwriter, Doris Akers, are true, "You can't beat God's giving, no matter how hard you try" (1958).

Think About It 🗩

The Search

"What are you now seeking?

What are you earnestly praying for?

Over what injustice are you anticipating that good will triumph?"

The answers to these questions are your lost coins.

The Service

"Where can I best find my place in service?"

"How can I be a doer of the gospel?"

"What do I have to give that is needed by humanity?"

The Answer to Prayer

Start and maintain a prayer journal. Record the answered prayers in your life.

Thank God for His provision, protection, guidance, and faithfulness.

Pray diligently for someone who needs to be restored to a right relationship with God.

Run to tell others about the goodness of God and the answer to prayer.

The author believes that the apex of a woman's experience is that she might find joy.

Look at the diagram below. Explain how joy is a thread of continuity that runs through Faith, Hope, Agapé Love, and Wisdom, the topics in this book.

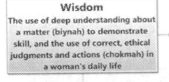

Wisdom
The use of deep understanding about a matter (biynah) to demonstrate skill, and the use of correct, ethical judgments and actions (chokmah) in a woman's daily life

Joy
Follows a woman's Search and her Service. Joy occurs when a woman experiences deep satisfaction over answered prayer, recovering what has been lost, seeing good triumph over evil; occurs when a woman is engaged in service

Love
Unwavering display of acceptance toward those who are in need; the bedrock of human needs, unconditional acceptance; often shown by women who raise children that they did not birth

Hope
Joyful anticipation of a bright future and pleasant outcome; often shown by those who expect the best at the birth of a child.

Faith
The substance of things hoped for; the evidence of things unseen; often seen as the hand of God, healing those who are sick.

Extend

Multiplying one's influence by use of their skills was an attribute that was also demonstrated by Tabitha, also called Dorcas. Tabitha was a skilled seamstress who was known for sewing garments for the widows and other townspeople in Joppa.

Tabitha (Dorcas) carried out the ministry of provision, nurture, and charity to those who were in need. When she died, the people of Joppa mourned deeply, as shown in the following passage of scripture:

36 Now there was at Joppa a certain disciple named Tabitha, which by interpretation is called Dorcas: this woman was full of good works and almsdeeds which she did.

37 And it came to pass in those days, that she was sick, and died: whom when they had washed, they laid her in an upper chamber.

39 . . . When he [Peter] was come, they brought him into the upper chamber: and all the widows stood by him weeping, and shewing the coats and garments which Dorcas made, while she was with them. Acts 9: 36-41

We can trust God to reward our faithfulness to Him with joy that others may not comprehend. This will give us a peace that passes all understanding.

* * *

BIBLE PROMISE FOR YOU

He will give you a peace that passes all understanding.
Philippians 4:7

ENDNOTE

1 Discussion of the Declaration of Independence was based on the document found at: http://www.heritage.org/initiatives/first-principles/primary-sources/the-declaration-of-independence

2 Herod Agrippa was the King referred to by the simple title, Herod, in Acts 12. Verified in http://en.wikipedia.org/wiki/Herod

3 In Acts 12:13, Bible records Mary's surname was Mark, hence Mary Mark:

> 13 [Peter] came to the house of Mary, the mother of John whose surname was Mark; where many were gathered together, praying.

Mary Mark was the mother of John Mark, who later joined the ministry of Saul and Barnabas. You can read about Mary Mark and her son John Mark in Acts 12:13 and Acts 12:25).

A company of believers were gathered at Mary Mark's house one night for intercessory prayer on behalf of the imprisoned Peter.

REFERENCES

Bible Gateway, www.biblegateway.com

http://www.biblegateway.com/passage/?search=luke%20 15&version=KJV

Blue Letter Bible. "Dictionary and Word Search for (Strong's (2212)."

Blue Letter Bible. 1996-2013, accessed from http://www.blbclassic. org/lang/lexicon/lexicon.cfm?Strongs=G2212&t=KJV

Definition and Usage of the Word, "Culminated," accessed from http:// dictionary.reference.com/browse/culminated?s=t

Declaration of Independence accessed from http://www.ushistory. org/declaration/

http://www.heritage.org/initiatives/first-principles/ primary-sources/the-declaration-of-independence

http://www.history.com/topics/declaration-of-independence

http://en.wikipedia.org/wiki/Herod